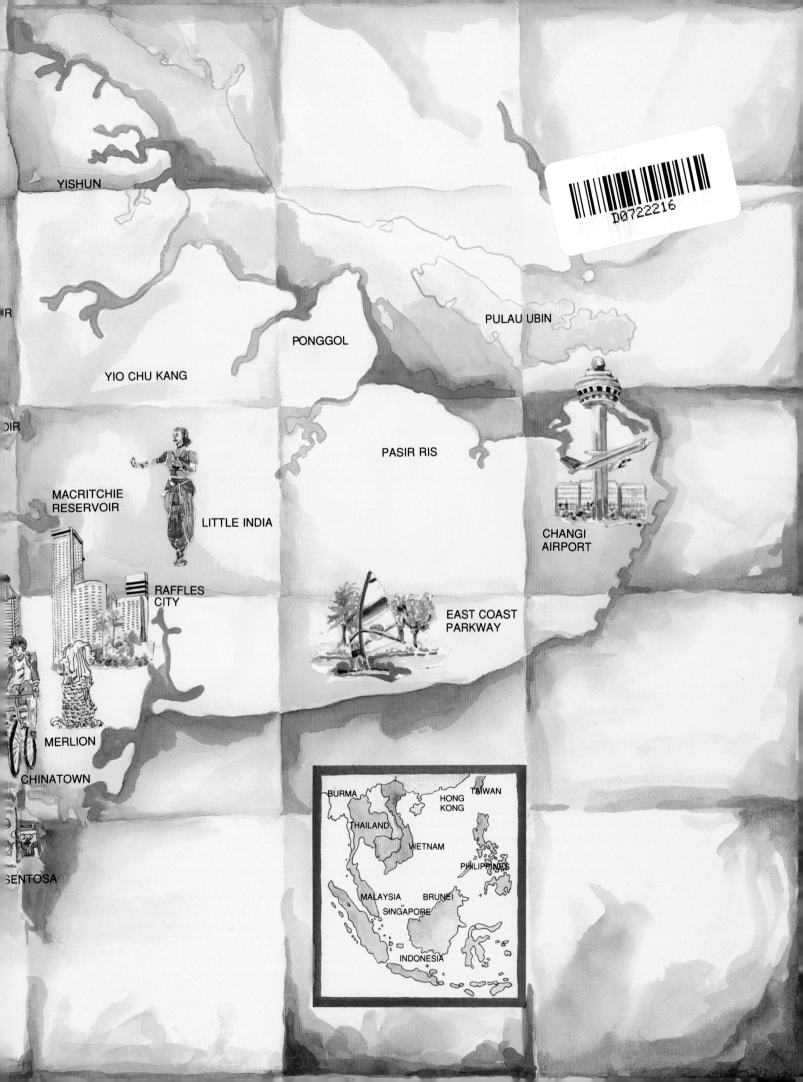

YISHUN

R

PULAU UBIN

PONGGOL

YIO CHU KANG

DIR

PASIR RIS

MACRITCHIE
RESERVOIR

LITTLE INDIA

CHANGI
AIRPORT

RAFFLES
CITY

EAST COAST
PARKWAY

MERLION

CHINATOWN

SENTOSA

BURMA

TAIWAN

HONG
KONG

THAILAND

VIETNAM

PHILIPPINES

MALAYSIA

BRUNEI

SINGAPORE

INDONESIA

Photographs in this book are available for re-use in magazines, brochures and advertising etc. from the library of:
R. Ian Lloyd Productions
5 Kreta Ayer Road
Singapore 088983
Tel: (65) 227-9600
Fax: (65) 227-9363

Production supervision by BSSCO Tech Enterprise.

Typesetting by Superskill Graphics

Colour separations by Daylight Colour Art

Printed in Singapore by Tien Wah Press Pte. Ltd.

ISBN No. 981-00-2225-5
Fourth edition 1997.

COVER: Statue of Sir Stamford Raffles at the place on the Singapore River where he landed in 1819, now eclipsed by the gleaming office towers of Raffles Place.

ENDPAPERS: Watercolour map of Singapore by Jorine Kok Mee Hong of Temasek Polytechnic, winner of a design class map competition.

HALF TITLE PAGE: National Day celebrations draw a wide assortment of Singapore faces each August.

FULL TITLE PAGE: Dragon motifs on the roof of Sin Ming Buddhist Temple.

CONTENTS PAGE: Pulau Seking island off the west coast.

PAGES 6-7: The Tanjong Pagar Restoration Area against a backdrop of Shenton Way and the financial district.

PAGES 8-9: Participants make waves at the 25th anniversary Jubilee Spectacular at the National Stadium.

PAGES 10-11: Early morning along the Singapore River, with the old shophouses of Boat Quay on the opposite shore.

PAGES 12-13: Muslims congregate for Friday prayers at Woodlands Mosque.

PAGES 14-15: Panorama of the Singapore River and the financial district from the top of the Westin Stamford, the world's tallest hotel.

PAGES 16-17: Teochew opera is popular at Chinese festivals.

SINGAPORE
State Of The Art

SINGAPORE
STATE OF THE ART

PHOTOGRAPHY BY R. IAN LLOYD • EDITED BY JOSEPH R. YOGERST
DESIGNED BY RONNIE TAN

WITH CONTRIBUTIONS BY ZURAIDAH IBRAHIM, GRETCHEN LIU,
VIOLET OON, ADRIAN TAN, RAVI VELOO AND PAUL ZACH

CONTENTS

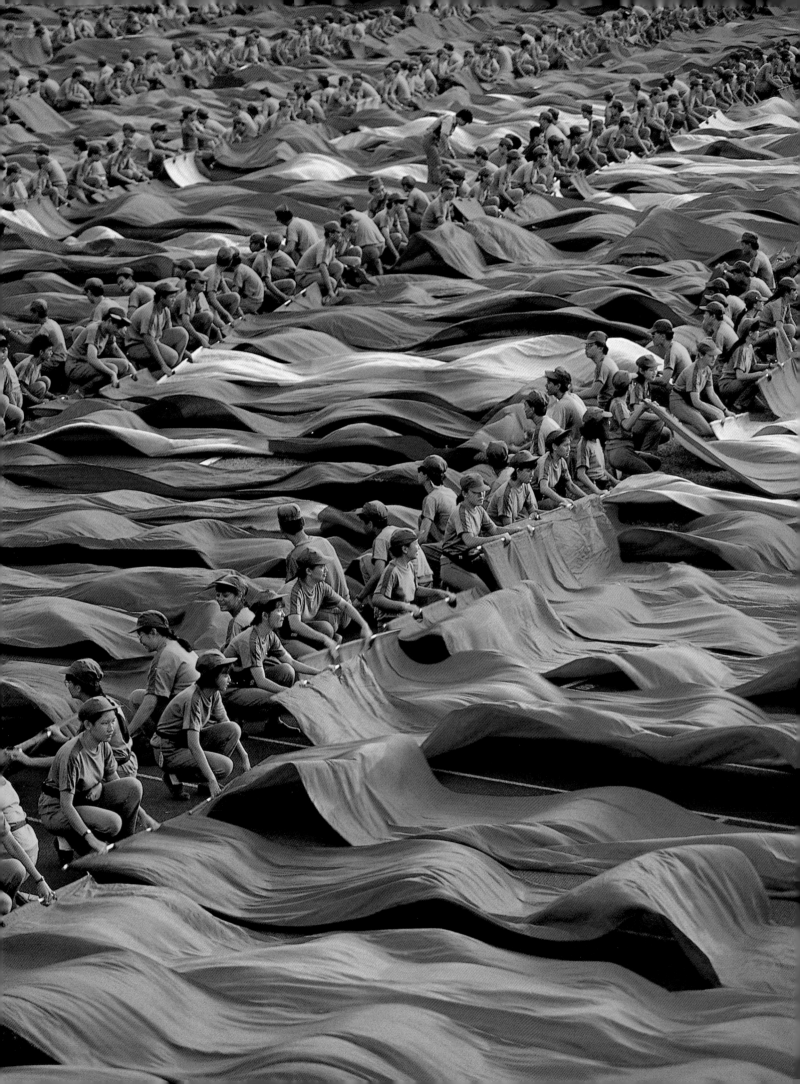

SINGAPORE WORKS!

WRITTEN BY PAUL ZACH

A satellite dish looms above the Bukit Timah Expressway, both emblematic of Singapore's heavy emphasis on infrastructure development in the last 25 years, part of the nations's overall push to develop its economy. The telecommunications network is considered the most sophisticated in Southeast Asia. Six-lane superhighways now crisscross the island.

Not long after I first set foot in Singapore, I slid into the back seat of an air-conditioned taxi owned and operated by Mr Tan Peck Kwan. Plastered on the back of the front seat was a plethora of posters, a full semester's worth of instructional primers governing the complex system of fares and surcharges and call bookings and more. And for good measure, there were even a few government campaign posters: Speak Mandarin, Make Courtesy Our Way of Life, Don't Spit, etc.

Most arresting, however, was a hand-lettered notice obviously the handiwork of Mr Tan himself. It read:

- Indicate early your precise alighting location.
- Do not place wet articles on the cushion.
- Ask for plastic bag if you are likely to vomit.
- Thank you. Happy travelling.

In their own unwitting way, Mr Tan's principles for ensuring the peace and comfort of his passengers sums up Singapore's ongoing prescription for curing the economic and social ills of its turbulent past. Until recently, trauma was an integral part of Singapore's modern history: the Japanese Occupation of World War II, the Communist threat and bloody riots of the 1950s, and finally merger and separation from Malaysia in the 1960s. Overcoming the stigma of those events called for an equally jolt-

Singapore harbour is a melange of tankers, container ships, oil drilling platforms, tugboats and even a few old Chinese-style craft. In 1990, the island passed Rotterdam as the world's busiest container port; construction of a new container terminal on Brani Island ensures that position is held. Also being built is a new passenger terminal at the World Trade Centre that will be able to serve the world's largest cruise ships.

ing regimen of rehabilitation. Only then could Singapore hope to get on the road to success. The political course would have to be precise and unwavering. Anti-social behaviour could not be tolerated. Convulsions would have to be contained.

Those, in a nutshell, were the rules for a smooth ride laid down by the man in the driver's seat when Singapore became an independent republic in 1965. The driver in this case was a Cambridge graduate who had scored an exceptional double-first degree in law with a star for distinction. His fellow students called him Harry Lee. When he became a politician, he reverted to his Chinese name, Kuan Yew — "The Light that Shines".

As the sun set on the 1970s — Singapore's first full decade of nationhood — it was obvious that Mr Lee Kuan Yew had produced a potent formula for nation-building. Though often at odds with his

methods, the foreign press had already conceded that he had worked an "economic miracle".

I arrived in 1978 as an eager, young journalist. Drawings at the immigration checkpoint indicated that men with hair extending over their collars were not welcome. As a former long-haired, bearded, anti-war student in America, I felt more than a little out of place. But that first taxi ride into Singapore proved humbling. While growing up in Cleveland, I had watched self-serving politicians ravage my middle American home. Yet rising before me on the other side of the globe, on a Southeast Asian island no larger than metropolitan Cleveland, was a prosperous city-state of staggering efficiency and immense scope. Perhaps Mr Lee and his ministers did rule with an iron rod, but they were prudent about it. And they got results.

At that time, a few rusting black taxis still lurched and rumbled through Singapore's scrubbed streets. Stuffing emerged from their stained seats while electric fans clamped to the dashboards swished at the torpid air, forcing you to lunge for the window

ABOVE LEFT: **Computer manufacture and design has become a major Singapore industry since the early 1980s. High-tech factories bring over a billion dollars a year to the Singapore economy. Among compo-** **nents produced here are microchips, disk drives, printers, circuit boards and transistors.**

Macintosh computer units being tested at the Apple factory in Singapore. Most of the big international computer firms have plants here including IBM, Unisys, Hewlett-Packard, Nixdorf and Data General. Most of the manufacture is for export, but on the home front seventy percent of the island's business firms are plugged into information technology — one of the globe's highest rates of computer penetration.

Action is fast and furious on the floor of SIMEX — the Singapore International Monetary Exchange, a popular financial futures market. Singapore has grown rapidly into a major financial node, with Asia's first "floorless" fully-computerized stock market, plus gold, oil futures and government securities markets, as well as more than 137 banks.

— only to have the handle fall off in your hands. But with squeaky-clean taxis like Mr Tan's starting to proliferate, the days of the clunkers were numbered.

Decay inferred poverty and simply could not be permitted. It was being rooted out in every corner of the city. The government pulled down picturesque but obsolete old shophouses in Chinatown, replacing them with anonymous but functional new residential blocks. Along Orchard Road, private developers bulldozed rows of quaint, slate-roofed stores with facades of painted tiles. In their place rose boxy, undistinguished shopping centres and hotels. Tourists, looking to impress their relatives with snapshots of the exotic Orient, lamented the disappearance of Singapore's "character" and colourful districts — but then, they didn't have to live in them.

While researching a story for *The Washington Post* in 1980, I interviewed the late Alex Josey, biographer and longtime press secretary to Prime Minister Lee. He explained Singapore's apparent lack of nostalgia for old buildings at that time: "Those buildings may attract tourists and look quaint on the outside, but they are unsanitary and unsafe inside. Besides, Singaporeans would rather not be reminded of the poverty of their past under British rule."

Josey had come to live in Singapore 35 years earlier when, he explained, he visited rooms above shops that housed as many as sixty people in six-foot cubicles without toilets or running water. "It's better to tear down the shophouses," he said, "so the government has the room to continue its remarkable programme of constructing public housing."

Singapore's policy of providing decent, affordable public housing may be the government's

Changi International, which replaced the old Paya Lebar field in 1981, is often named in surveys as the world's best designed and most efficient airport. Changi doubled its potential capacity to 24 million passengers per year with the addition of ultra-modern Terminal Two in 1990. More than 52 carriers link Singapore to 110 cities in 54 countries. The Singapore girl (RIGHT) has become an ubiquitous symbol of Singapore Airlines' own global success.

most awesome achievement. In 1960, there were 1,682 flats in government-built estates. By the 1990s, there were some 700,000 government flats, housing nearly 90 per cent of Singapore 2.7 million population.

Residents of these estates used to jokingly refer to their flats as "matchboxes" and "pigeon holes" because most were small and one looked just like the next. But as the immediate need to provide a roof over the head of each family neared fulfillment in the 1980s, their tune changed. The government actually started to demolish or gut old flat blocks — some barely a decade old. Existing units were enlarged and a range of units with varying floor plans was built; stylish design touches enhanced each block. Some new towns got country-club style community centres with swimming pools and other facilities.

LEFT: The East Coast Parkway flows over Benjamin Sheares Bridge, linking two of the island's more important reclamation projects — Marina Square and Marina South. Landfill projects have allowed Singapore to expand significantly outwards from its modest natural base. Reclaimed land is now used for factories, oil refineries, container terminals, ship-yards, condominiums, hotels, shopping malls, food centres, parks and beaches. RIGHT: Shenton Way and the financial district as seen from the top of the OUB building, Singapore's highest at 280 metres. Further along the waterfront is the bustling Tanjong Pagar Container Terminal.

Today, some public housing units could pass for posh condominiums — even in the West.

The comprehensive transport network that links these burgeoning satellite towns to the city centre is another impressive achievement. When I first came to Singapore, there were no superhighways. Within a decade there were four expressways covering nearly a hundred kilometres, two more under construction and three more on the drawing board. Meanwhile, large fleets of buses — including a number that are air conditioned — link the housing estates to one another.

Even more remarkable was a project that got underway in October 1983: Singapore broke ground for a $5-billion, 67-kilometre Mass Rapid Transit (MRT) system with 42 stations. Despite the complexity of the project — about a third of it was to be underground or beneath rivers — the first five stations opened four years later. Within seven years, the entire system was up and running, serving roughly 800,000 passengers each day.

It seemed a hard-nosed, hard working population driven by a tough taskmaster could produce results — quickly. The foresight and resolve displayed by Mr Lee was obviously another factor. During a visit to Washington in 1975, he received a cable from home advising that construction of a new airport at Changi was feasible as long as expansion continued at the old airport at Paya Lebar. Mr Lee didn't hesitate. The next day he cabled his permission to proceed — even though it would mean writing off some $800 million in new investments at Paya Lebar and spending another $2 billion on the new airport.

Changi International opened in 1981. Before the end of the decade, seasoned travellers were calling Changi the world's best airport in magazine surveys and it had become such a major transportation hub that a second terminal was required. Finished in late 1990, Terminal II will help increase airport capacity from 14 to 24 million passenger per year. Not coincidentally, the rise of Singapore's national air carrier parallel that of the airport. By 1990, Singapore Airlines was flying Megatop 747s to London and Los Angeles, had one of the world's best safety records — and seasoned travellers were calling it the world's best airline in magazine surveys.

Meanwhile, the construction of significant new buildings in the city centre accelerated. Raffles City was anchored by the world's tallest hotel — the 71- storey Westin Plaza. Even taller was OUB Centre, in the expanding Raffles Place financial district. Sino-American architect I.M. Pei's Gateway complex soared above Beach Road.

Furthermore, the government earmarked several pockets of historic buildings for restoration rather than demolition. Shophouses in Tanjong Pagar have been transformed into stylish offices, boutiques, restaurants and tea houses. Colonial buildings were also restored: Empress Place got a facelift and new life as a museum. The crowning achievement was the $200-million restoration of the fabled 19th-century Raffles Hotel into a posh all-suites establishment.

Meanwhile, Singapore also took advantage of its vaunted maritime legacy. State-of-the-art docking and container facilities continued to expand and made Singapore the world's busiest port in terms of tonnage and containers by the early 1990s.

And keeping it all working with precision was an increasingly sophisticated infrastructure, including one of the world's most advanced telecommunications networks. Indeed, Singapore seemed impatient to get on with the 21st century more than a decade ahead of the rest of the world.

Two symbols of national pride are extensive public housing and the efficient Mass Rapid Transit (MRT) system. More than ninety percent of the island's 2.7 million people live in Housing Development Board (HDB) flats, over 700,000 total units. They are linked to the city centre by the 67 kilometres of MRT track that carry 800,000 commuters per day. The last link was completed in 1990, as the MRT project came in more than two years ahead of schedule and fifteen percent under budget.

CHAPTER TWO

CHINESE LIFE: OF OBIANG AND KIASU

WRITTEN BY ADRIAN TAN

A young woman sips Pepsi in front of the Thian Hock Keng Temple. Singapore's Chinese have synthesized their traditional religion and traditions with modern pop cultural and high-tech innovations to create a hybrid society that is unlike any other in Asia.

There is more to being a Singapore Chinese than being Singaporean and Chinese. To begin with, the Singapore Chinese, like the mule, is an impossible hybrid: the offspring of a high-tech island-state and a 6000-year-old culture.

The reason, of course, lies in the unnatural selection of the Chinese species a hundred years ago. In the 19th century, the first Chinese set foot on this island. Those ground-breaking immigrants were not scholars, or priests, or nobles, or government officials. They were either the Chinese lower-middle class (merchants, shopkeepers) or the workers (coolies, cooks, artisans and the odd prodigal son fleeing from justice in the best Chinese traditions).

Because of his unique heritage the modern Singapore Chinese is a wonderful chop suey of contradictions: ultra-pragmatic, yet super-duperstitious. . . fatalistic, yet ambitious. . . authoritarian, yet rebellious. And his cosmopolitan present and his provincial past have cross-bred to spawn two uniquely Singaporean quirks: *obiangism* and *kiasuism*.

Basically, *obiangism* concerns itself with ostentatious displays of bad taste. However, in true Singaporean over-achieving fashion, *obiang* bad taste is not bad taste of the common or garden variety, but bad taste par excellence — spectacular, high-class bad taste. Some classic examples of *obiangism* include mock-jade, Greco-Roman pillars on the porch of a semi-detached terrace house, or a screaming red Mercedes Benz with gold-plated bumpers, rims and star insignia.

Obiangism is easily explained. Singapore-Chinese are perhaps the most nouveau of the nouveau riche. Success in Singapore is still quantitative, not qualitative. Aesthetic appreciation is neglected, and instead value is placed on high price.

On the other hand, *kiasuism* is defined as a pathological fear of losing even the most minute of advantages. Thus, the typical *kiasu* will avidly compete in three Great National Sports:

(1) The 100-metre taxi hurdles: participants leap-frog each other down crowded streets in the direction of approaching traffic. The first to hail a cab wins. No handicaps are awarded to the old, the pregnant or the infirm.

(2) The theatre sitting high-jump: participants endeavour to out jump each other as soon as a play, concert or film reaches its conclusion. The first ones to reach the car park wins. Losers get to watch the screen credits and resuscitate badly mauled feet.

(3) Synchronized streaming: two teams participate. One arrives inside a vehicle (usually a bus or MRT train) while the other waits outside. As the doors open both groups begin forcing their way in or out. Tripping is permitted.

The origins of *kiasuism* again lie in recent history. Our immigrant forefathers were hungry. They underwent many lean decades, and even the Japanese Occupation, before the current years of plenty. A national insecurity complex developed, leading to *kiasuism*.

These twin traits are most obvious when the Singapore Chinese deals with the subjects closest to his heart, viz, the infamous Four Fs: festivals, food, family and sex.

The Chinese love to celebrate festivals, partly because it gives them a chance to be with the family, but mostly because it gives them an excuse to eat.

LEFT: **Trishaws parked in a Chinatown alley. Numerous trishaws still ply the streets of Singapore; they cater primarily to the tourist trade, but some locals continue to use them for short hops.**

ABOVE: **Early morning in Chinatown, a trishaw driver shaves at home before another day on the road.**

Sin Ming Temple in Ang Mo Kio. This is a major venue for Vesak Day celebrations in May to mark the three great events in the life of the Lord Buddha: birth, enlightenment and death. Devotees crowd the temple precinct on Vesak Day, bearing offerings, lighting joss sticks and praying before the various alters. Sin Ming is also home to a community of saffron-robbed Buddhist monks.

Lunar New Year is the most important Chinese festival. The ancient story behind this celebration concerns a huge monster (the Nien) who terrorized Chinese villagers. It was eventually discovered that this beast could be kept at bay by two things: the colour red and very loud noises. This led to a "hue and cry" approach to fighting the Nien. The hue (red) was worn on the annual occasion of the Nien's visitations. Small children were also given small red packets (or *hongbao*) to ward off the evil monster. To prevent their offspring from losing these *hongbao,* parents placed coins inside the packets. The cries were soon replaced by the sound of exploding firecrackers.

In Singapore, the traditions of Chinese New Year have developed along predictable lines. The more *kiasu* among Singapore-Chinese have abandoned the idea of giving coins to their children at New Year: coins are trivial and suggest poverty. However, one may gain an important social advantage by dishing out large denominations of currency. Thus the *hongbao* of today are more likely to be filled with crisp new $50 or $100 bills.

In addition, it's a common superstition that the Kitchen God (one of the hundreds of deities the Chinese worship) returns to heaven every New Year to report on the behaviour of the family. A good

RIGHT: A spirit medium strikes a distinct simian pose during a trance in which the Monkey God takes control of his body. The medium's job — in his transformation into the Monkey God — is to dispense assistance and advice to Taoist worshippers. The Monkey God's birthday is celebrated twice each year — in February and October — during which time a carnival atmosphere prevails at his temples, with performances of opera, puppet shows and acrobatics.

report prompts heaven to look kindly on the family. Instead of behaving well, however, the Chinese family simply smears the mouth of the idol with honey, a literal "sweetener" to ensure that the Kitchen God speaks well of the family. Are the Chinese the only race who believe that even gods may be bribed?

Another popular occasion is the Rice Dumpling Festival. Originally, this event was to commemorate the death of a famous Chinese patriot who decided to end his life by jumping into the Yellow River. In vain, his countrymen set out in long dragon boats to search for his body. They subsequently decided to discourage the fish from feeding on the corpse by tossing rice dumplings into the river.

In Singapore, the Chinese have concluded that this custom merely results in the waste of some perfectly good dumplings. Thus, the tradition today is that living mortals consume the dumplings while the fish go hungry. And what of the dragon boats? Well, they are still raced on our waters — a colourful tourist attraction that's good for business.

But the quintessential Singapore-Chinese festival is still Ching Ming. On this day, we visit the graves of our ancestors, do a little maintenance work with a broom and a lawn-mower, and then — surprise! surprise! — eat. The dead, of course, are offered a portion of the victuals, just as they are offered many other items during their funerals.

In the past, Chinese people gave "hell money" to their dead. This consisted of paper (yes, we invented that) folded in the shape of gold or silver ingots, or simply printed to look like paper money (yes, we invented that as well), subsequently burnt so that the dead could resolve their liquidity problems at the big Restaurant In The Sky.

Nowadays, Singapore Chinese have added some notoriously *obiang* innovations. Instead of mere paper money, mourners can be seen burning paper credit cards (Amex Gold, no less), paper BMWs (our current transport of delight), paper mobile phones and three-storey paper mansions with kidney-shaped pools and the proverbial kitchen sink. Pragmatically, we Chinese believe that you *can* take it with you.

LEFT: During the Lantern Festival on the 15th night of the eight moon (in late September or early October), children gather in colourful costumes at the Chinese Garden in Jurong. Tradition says this is the night when "magicians touch the moon." To celebrate, the Chinese eat mooncakes made from red beans and lotus nuts, and display ornate lanterns — often in the shape of animals, boats and aeroplanes.

Chinese students gather for the annual National Day celebration on 9th August. Singapore's Chinese crave special occasions, for these are ideal times to combine their favourite obsessions: family and food. Several dozen Chinese festivals dot the Singapore calendar, from Lunar New Year in January or February to the Festival of the Nine Emperor Gods in October or November.

LEFT: A Chinese geomancer, astrologer and palmist holds aloft his astrological compass. BELOW Thian Hock Keng Temple on Telok Ayer Street in Chinatown is one of Singapore's oldest places of Taoist worship. Dedicated to Ma Chu Po, goddess of the sea, the complex was built in 1841 along what was then the waterfront, with funds provided by appreciative sailors who had been spared calamities at sea. The overall effect is Chinese, but the temple also incorporates Scottish ironwork and Dutch tiles. BOTTOM: Fierce door gods painted on the entrance to Thian Hock Keng.

But food is really the great national pastime. A positive feeding frenzy ensues at every Chinese feast. But like most Chinese rituals, there are strict rules of etiquette to observe:

ARRIVAL: most guests arrive at a dinner late. This is not discourtesy, but extreme courtesy, as the diners do not wish to appear greedy. As a rule, 30 minutes is "fashionably polite" — unless the dinner invitation includes the word "sharp" (e.i. 8.15 "sharp", in which case one should appear at 8.25).

THE TABLE: most Chinese eat at a round table. This isn't due to any tradition of egalitarianism (a very un-Chinese concept). The table is round because:

(a) the Chinese enjoy the shape, as it suggests continuity and longevity;

(b) conversation is encouraged, as diners need not shout at each other across a long table. Nevertheless, this has not prevented most Chinese dinners, even the most formal ones, from sounding like the trading floor of the Singapore Monetary Exchange;

(c) the guest of honour must sit within a chopstick's reach of his host. This is because the dinner traditionally commences with the host depositing a choice portion of food from the central dish onto the guest's plate.

THE DISHES: diners are not served individual

portions. Instead, they are expected to obtain nourishment from a dish of food placed at the centre of the table. Furthermore, the more important the occasion, the more courses will be served. Usually, there are 12 dishes, beginning with the "cold dish" (chicken, *pei-tan* or century egg, prawns and seaweed are favourites) and ending with a sweet dessert.

Extravagance is also a good measure of how important the dinner function is. Usually, an expansive host will treat his guests to *obiang* cuisine. These dishes are usually never to be found in mainland China, because the ingredients — bear's paw or tiger's testicles — are as rare as the animals themselves.

Among the more *obiang* local delicacies are live monkey's brain (now banned), live deep-fried carp (also banned), drunken prawns and the quaint,

RIGHT: Final touches are applied to a traditional Baba wedding costume amid the splendour of an old-time Straits Chinese wedding chamber in the Peranakan Place Museum. LEFT: Yet brides with a modern orientation usually opt for a white Western-style wedding dress and photo session in the Chinese Garden. Arranged marriages were once a fact of life in Chinese society; today most young people choose their own mates.

admittedly delicious, *yu-sheng*. The latter is, in fact, raw fish, a must every New Year. Singapore Chinese enjoy tossing this salad of fish, vegetables and nuts as the description of this activity (tossing the raw fish) can also be happily punned into the phrase "More Prosperity for Business".

(Here we also see the Chinese people's notorious addiction to puns. In fact, the *obiang* manifestation of this punning can be seen in our car licence plates. Whereas in the West, personalized licence plates are sought after because of the Westerner's obsession with identity — thus we see many names and nicknames on these plates — in Singapore, personalized licence plates are used as lucky totems. So a rich businessman may pay up to $100,000 for the "8888" licence number, as this can be punned into four-squared "prosperity" in Cantonese.)

Chinese family hierarchy is very rigid, with strict divisions according age and sex. Unlike youth-conscious Westerners, the Chinese enjoy being considered old. Age confers seniority. Seniority implies experience. Experience brings wisdom. Wisdom demands respect. And where would we be without respect? Here are some important people in a typical Chinese family:

THE MOTHER: the object of 99 per cent of filial love, she is bestowed with god-like status.

THE FATHER: the supreme authority on everything from matchmaking to running the family business, to why we should not go out next Saturday as it looks like rain. He aspires to a god-like status.

THE ELDEST SON: the future. Old-fashioned Chinese still believe that males are better than females. The son will carry on the family name, while the daughter will be married off to somebody else's household. Thus, the son most often imagines he has god-like status.

THE GRANDFATHER: the patriarch. He is usually indulgent and doting, especially to his grandchildren. He has some vestigial demi-god-like status.

THE ANCESTORS: since most Chinese still practice ancestor worship, it would not be too outrageous to suggest that these ancient ones are all gods.

To have families, one must have sex. But the Chinese, one of the most conservative of races, are especially reticent when it comes to this topic. Until recently, most Chinese were matchmade by their parents and grandparents. Matchmaking criteria included the wealth of the prospective in-laws and their social standing within the community. In these deliberations, "love" became a four-letter word.

Of course, sex education was taboo. The idea was that young women could only be married off if their chastity was preserved. Thus even dating was forbidden, as this led to suspicions of impropriety. A case of *kiasuism* on the part of the parents? As a marvellous tribute to contradictory thinking, the young girl — who was forbidden contact with any males throughout her life — was expected to give herself to a total stranger (the matchmade husband) on their wedding night.

Thankfully, today, most young Singapore-Chinese have taken to choosing their own life-mates, sometimes even against their parents violent objections. Still, sex education and sexual knowledge are only furtively discussed.

As Singapore matures, so will the Singapore-Chinese. Like acne, or milk teeth, *obiangism* and *kiasuism* will be outgrown. Superstitions will be forgotten. The Singapore-Chinese will become socially perfect.

And to think, it might only take a few centuries.

LEFT: Chinese students practice tae kwon do, a martial art imported from Korea. Other martial arts such as karate and judo are also popular in Singapore, as is *tai chi*, a traditional Chinese exercise routine that is often called "shadow boxing". ABOVE: Qigong Shi Ba Shi — the 18 Movement Exercise Display — immensely popular at housing estates, especially at dawn.

CHAPTER THREE

THE MALAY EXPERIENCE

WRITTEN BY ZURAIDAH IBRAHIM

Three generations of a Malay family sit on their front doorstep in Geylang Serai. Malays comprise about fifteen percent of Singapore's population and the vast majority are Muslims. In many respects, they are still trying to come to terms with the transition from life in the traditional *kampung* villages to high-rise apartment blocks.

Sitting on the concrete-and-mosaic bench under the void deck of her son's flat, betel leaves staining her lips a deep red, a leathery old lady surveys her surroundings wearily and sighs. It has been some 14 years since she left her beloved *kampung* in Geylang Serai for this concrete Bedok habitat, all in the name of modernization and progress. There is much to be said about living in a Housing Development Board (HDB) flat, she murmurs quietly to herself. She likes the cool plastered walls, the sleek sanitation, the fancy gadgets that give off light and heat, and the spacious rooms. But still, the *kampung* spirit is hard to replace, she declares decidedly.

Old Mak Timah is probably not alone in feeling this way. However, younger Malays with more energy — like Mak Timah's son — are trying to bring something of the essence of the old *kampung* to life in the modern city. For instance, her son has helped organize a Muslim block committee, where the able-bodied among the Malay men form a loose club to oversee communal functions. They ensure that events such as common prayers, *kenduris,* burial ceremonies, *berkhatan* (circumcision) and weddings are carried out without any hitches. The block committee is really a carryover of the *gotong-royong* (mutual help) spirit that was an essential part of traditional village life that Mak Timah seems to miss so much.

Most of Singapore's *attap* (thatched) *kampungs* — with their high-peaked houses, swaying coconut palms and backyard vegetable patches — have been systematically levelled by the bulldozer and the villagers resettled in HDB estates since independence in 1965. In fact, only one true *kampung* remains: on Pulau Seking island, where about 200 Malays cling to their bygone lifestyles. The rest have been absorbed into the speedy Singapore mainstream. Yet the Malays remained a close-knit community where religious festivals and celebrations play a central, unifying role in life. The block committee represents one attempt at retaining solidarity.

Malays make up about 15 per cent of Singapore's population and almost all of them are Muslims. The mosque remains a fundamental commu-

nal amenity in the Muslim community. All working Muslims voluntarily contribute a monthly minimum sum of one dollar to the Mosque Building Fund which is used to help finance the construction of new mosques in housing estates. Since its inception in 1975, the fund has financed eleven mosques, with five others nearing completion. Another five are on the drawing board. These mosques have modern facilities such as computers and multi-purpose rooms, plus contemporary designs to complement the new towns which they serve.

Yet perhaps the grandest religious structure in Singapore is the old Sultan Mosque, on North Bridge Road in the hub of what was once a thriving Malay-Arab business community. The building represents a quaint mixture of Classical, Persian, Moorish

RIGHT: **Kampong Glam and the Sultan Mosque are brightly lit during the annual Hari Raya celebrations that mark the end of the month-long period of prayer and fasting called Ramadan. During Hari Raya, Malays dress in their finest new clothes and visit the homes of their friends and relatives, where special feasts are prepared.** ABOVE: **Friday prayers inside Sultan Mosque.**

and Turkish design themes. Built in 1824, it's currently undergoing a S$3-million facelift to restore and extend its premises. Less known, but just as historic, is the Hajjah Fatimah mosque near Beach Road. It was commissioned in 1845 by a rich businesswoman from Malacca who married a Bugis trader and settled down in Kampong Glam.

Indeed, Kampong Glam was the residence of many prominent Malay personalities during and after the Raffles era. In fact, it was officially allocated to the Malays and Muslims in Raffles' famous town plan of 1822. The district takes its name from the glam trees that grew in the area then, and which

Although the Lantern Festival is a Chinese celebration, Malay children often dress up and enter the costume competition at the Chinese Garden.

were a source of planking timber and bark for caulking. The Malays — who were here when Raffles landed in 1819, and whose numbers swelled as they were joined by others from Malacca and other parts of Malaya, Sumatra and the Riau-Lingga archipelago — also settled along Singapore's coast and the smaller offshore islands. They were later joined by others of almost similar heritage: the Javanese, Baweanese and Bugis from what is now Indonesia.

Malays still gather in Kampong Glam, especially during Ramadan, the fasting month, to buy dates, *murtabak* (fried bread stuffed with mutton and onions) and a sumptuous spread of mouth-watering Malay delicacies for the breaking of fast. The shops along Arab Street still stock lavish velvet, satin and silk for special outfits to be worn only during the special Hari Raya Aidil Fitri holiday, which is a time of rejoicing after Ramadan.

While religion plays a central role in a Malay's life, secular culture also remains a treasured pillar of his existence. But with resurgent Islam, many cultural traditions have been tailored to abide by Islamic injunctions. For example, some Malay/Muslim couples don't feel it is fitting in the eyes of Islam to grace the decorated dais, or *pelamin,* on their wedding day. Nowadays they might dispense with this aspect of their wedding, and no one really minds.

For others, Malay court culture is still very much evident today, as seen at traditional weddings. The Malay newlyweds are accorded royal treatment for a day. The couple — or "king" and "queen" — are adorned with fine *songket* (gold-embroidered cloth) and soft silks as they lead a procession of music and *silat* (martial arts) to the husband's house. The procession is accompanied by a musical group called the *hadrah,* whose members beat the kompang (a small hand drum) most heartily.

Before the couple can advance to the *pelamin,* there is the *akad nikah* or solemnization ceremony which is usually conducted at the bride's house.

ABOVE: **Some Malay school-girls still wear traditional Muslim veils as part of their uniform.** RIGHT: **A Malay woman practices** *silat,* **the traditional Malay martial art.**

During the *akad nikah,* marriage vows are recited according to Islamic law and then the couple exchange gifts. These can range from a simple prayer mat to more trendy treats such as designer watches or expensive French perfume.

After the official ceremony, the wedding takes on a more lively note. The couple sit on the *pelamin* and have their pictures taken with various relatives and friends, who toss saffron rice and rosewater to the bride and groom as signs of posterity and happiness. Guests at a Malay wedding never leave empty-handed. Traditionally they received a hard-boiled egg and glutinous saffron rice, but this has been modified to suit modern preferences and can now be sweets, chocolates or cakes.

To ensure that these and other traditions are not diluted by the tide of time, the Malay members of parliament and other community leaders hatched the idea of creating a living, breathing Malay village. Sprawling across a 1.4-hectare plot in Geylang Serai — the hub of Malay activity and formerly the site of one of Singapore's biggest *kampungs* — the Geylang Serai Malay Village promises to be a showcase of Malay culture and tradition. When it initially opened for a short time during and just after the Malay Cultural Month in February 1990, visitors were treated to demonstrations of Malay crafts such as batik-painting, cloth weaving, top-making and kite-making. There were special rooms used solely to display bridal artefacts and traditional kitchen ware, plus a cultural hall constructed of fine wood which will again be used to stage a variety of Malay perform-ances, such as the *dondang sayang,* the *joget* and *silat.*

But as Mak Timah's engineer grandson would be quick to point out, there is more to the Malay than simply culture. He can be just as dedicated and hardworking as his fellow Singaporeans. More and more Malays are venturing into the area of com-merce and industry. One proud example of their

LEFT: **Although the vast majority of Singapore's Muslims are of Malay descent, this devotee at Sultan Mosque is an Indian. Their ancestors hail from what is today Pakistan,**

Since its inception in 1975, the Mosque Building Fund, to which all working Muslims subscribe, has funded the construction of eleven mosques, including this modern structure in Ang Mo Kio, a massive new town at the centre of the island.

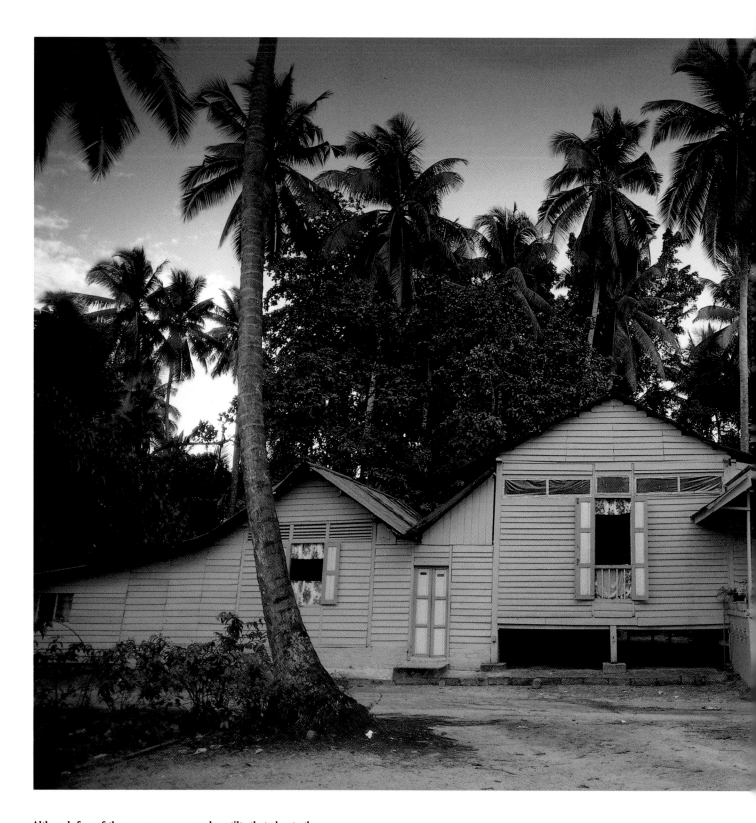

Although few of them now exist, the traditional Malay *kampung* house was once a popular form of accommodation. The intrinsic characteristics of the *kampung* style are clapboard sides, thatched or corrugated metal roof and wooden stilts that elevate the dwelling above water or land. This latter touch provides relief from floods and a cheap form of air conditioning, but also keeps snakes at bay.

increasing success is Second Chance, a chain of menswear shops owned by Malay entrepreneur Mohamed Salleh Marican.

Over the last two decades, there has emerged an expanding pool of well-educated Malays who serve as role models for young Malays trying to succeed in the education system. It's an acknowledged fact that Malays lag behind the other races in terms of classroom achievements. Still, various efforts in recent years have reaped positive results. For example, the Primary School Leaving Examinations, mathematics pass rate among Malay children rose from 31 per cent in 1982 to 45 per cent in 1989. Similarly, the proportion of Malay students with at least five "O" levels more than doubled, from 19 per cent in 1982 to 42 per cent in 1988.

Progress at these critical points of the education system still lag behind the national average — Malays are painfully aware of this. In many Malay homes today, the importance of education and how it can be utilized to change one's economic status is often stressed. Recognizing the need for a national effort to tackle this problem of poor educational performance among Malay children, the Malay community set up Mendaki, the Council for the Education of Muslim Children, in 1981. It ran weekend tuition classes, computer courses and family-based programmes. In 1989, the body was expanded to

RIGHT: Pulau Seking, a tiny island off the west coast, is the last of Singapore's true *kampungs*. The 200 residents cling stubbornly to old ways. Generators provide electricity while fresh water is hauled in jerry cans from nearby Pulau Bukom. Most of Seking's men work at the huge Shell refinery; children commute to school each day.

take on the socio-economic problems besetting the community.

The Malays know tough challenges lie ahead. They must ensure that they advance just as rapidly as the other races or they may be left behind. At the same time, within this framework, they must retain their bearings or risk becoming an alienated people. As the largest minority community in Singapore, they must also ponder problems of integration.

The Muslim block committee in Mak Timah's neighbourhood may look rather insular at first glance. But as some of these committees have shown, it can be the first step towards building bridges with other neighbourhood committees. A number of Muslim block committees members also serve on larger Residents' Committees — ample proof that Malays do want to be part of national life.

LEFT: A stationmaster for Singapore's only railway line, which runs from an Art Deco-style main station near Tanjong Pagar to Johor Bahru across the Causeway in Malaysia. The line, rolling stock and stations are still owned and operated by the Malaysian government as part of the overall peninsula railway network. ABOVE RIGHT: Malay man in traditional sarong leaves Friday prayers at Sultan Mosque. BOTTOM RIGHT: Malay girl at Singapore's 25th Anniversary Jubilee Spectacular at the National Stadium.

LEFT: Once a trademark of Singapore waters, kelongs are now a dying breed. The stilts around these man-made fish traps — made from nipah palms — are deployed in such a way as to channel fish into nets beneath the elevated hut during movements of the tide. But most kelongs have now been transformed into corporate fish farms. TOP: Malay fishermen anchor their tiny craft to mangrove trees north of Pulau Seking. ABOVE: Children splash in the sea off Seking's municipal pier.

CHAPTER FOUR

INDIAN SINGAPORE: A DIVERSITY OF UNITY

WRITTEN BY RAVI VELOO

Hindu priest in the courtyard of Sri Vadapathira Kaliamman Temple on Serangoon Road. Indians make up less than seven per cent of the population. Yet they are anything but a homogeneous group: they embrace the Hindu, Muslim, Sikh and Christian religions; they are Tamils, Keralans, Punjabis, Sindhis and Gujeratis. OVERLEAF: A goldsmith toils in his tiny shop in Little India.

The Indians. A vague term to describe a culturally diverse segment of Singapore's population. Nine out of ten of them were not even born in India, but here in Singapore; many have never set foot in the subcontinent that gives them their identity. They worship in Hindu temples, churches or mosques according to their religion. They speak and write different languages and wear distinctly different dress; they don't even eat the same food. About the only claim to common ground they may have is that somewhere up the genealogical tree, each and everyone of them should be able to trace an antecedent from the Indian subcontinent.

Nonetheless, the census will tell you that seven per cent of Singapore's population is Indian. What it means to be an Indian of a particular background becomes more obvious when one traces the history of the Indians here.

Among the first Indians to venture to the Malay Peninsula were merchants from the Coromandel coast of southern India. They brought cloth, iron tools, "magic" amulets and precious stones to trade for spices, tin, gold and ivory as far back as the 1st century AD. In those days, the sea journey depended a great deal on the direction of the monsoon winds, and Indian traders who travelled to the region remained only a few months before returning home.

Meanwhile, the traders set up base, travelled and learnt the native customs. Many married into local communities and Indian culture was assimilated into the local ways. In later centuries, the expansionist Sri Vijaya (650-1350) and Majapahit (1280-1500) empires swept through South East Asia, spreading the Hindu religion and leaving their mark on every facet of life. This gave the Indians an influence in the region far beyond their numbers. To what extent that influence spread to Singapore — or Temasek as it was known then — is a fact lost in time. But it is known that the name Singapore is derived from the

Sanskrit words, *singha* (lion) and *pura* (port).

There is some suggestion that the sacking of Temasek in 1365 by the Majapahit empire effectively ended the relationship between Indian traders and Singapore until Sir Stamford Raffles sought out the island in February 1819 to establish a new port. From his own account, it's plain that Singapore was a lost city to the Indians by then. Raffles wrote: "But for my Malay studies, I should hardly have known that such a place existed; not only the European but the Indian world was ignorant of it."

On Raffles' second trip to Singapore, a couple of months later, he brought along a few Indians from Penang. One of them was Naraina Pillai, who stayed and helped draw other Indians from Penang

Shades of the old country: religious posters for sale along Serangoon Road, the spine of Singapore's Indian community. Notice the mingling of Hinduism and Christianity — Jesus and the Virgin Mary blend easily with Shiva and Vishnu.

to help build Singapore's infrastructure. Indian merchants soon began arriving with the Chinese from Malacca, eager to seize the opportunities promised by a new and strategic colony, a deep water harbour and the world's first free port.

As word spread about the prosperous little island, now known as Singapore, more Indian merchants began arriving here, many of them direct from India. They established themselves in the harbour area around High Street, and also in Arab and Market streets, which even now retain elements of their Indian flavour. The High Street vendors in-

This sidewalk fortune teller in Little India employs the mystic intuition of a green parrot (in cage). After hearing the customer's vital details whispered into his ear, the bird picks from a deck of pink cards. The sage then determines the fortune by matching the card with texts from the ancient Hindu scriptures contained in his many books. Also on display is his official fortune teller's license.

cluded the north Indians — the Hindu Sindhis and the turbaned Sikhs — groups that comprise about six and eight per cent, respectively, of the Indian community today. As the number of traders grew, they were followed by those who provided other services, such as priests and skilled craftsmen.

A little remembered fact is that during the early colonial period, the Chettiars, a sub-caste from southern India, filled the vacuum for high-risk capital with their home-based money-lending operations. They financed risky projects that the big banks wouldn't touch, and some sources say the rubber plantations of Malaysia would not have succeeded without the high-risk capital of the Chettiars. Today, their biggest claim to fame is one of the oldest Hindu temples in Singapore, the Chettiars' Temple in Tank Road, and the colourful, enthralling and ritualistic Thaipusam festival.

To help them run the island-colony, the British also imported Indian civil servants from the sub-continent. Under British rule, English-educated Indians staffed the middle and lower rungs of the administration. As British subjects, they had political rights at a time when a largely migrant population in Singapore had little inclination to sink its roots here. These historical advantages were later to be reflected

LEFT: **The huge head of a Hindu god peers out the front door of a shrine at Sri Mariamman Temple on South Bridge Road during the Navarathiri Festival.** RIGHT: **A giant silver chariot passes the entrance to Chettiar Temple on Tank Road as part of the procession on the day before Thaipusam. During this annual festival, Hindu devotees skewer their faces and bodies with sharp metal hooks and pins; some bear heavy metal frames called kavadis on their shoulders as a sign of their faith.**

in the high profile of Indians in the early legislatures, trade unions, the professions and the civil service. Indeed, much of Singapore law is based on the Indian Penal Code.

Raffles also drew on convict labour from the sub-continent to build roads, buildings and public utilities. Just as Irish convicts were sent to Australia, Indian convicts were sent to Penang, Malacca and Singapore. Under Raffles' enlightened rule, the convicts — who were held in a prison near Serangoon Road — could farm their own land and settle down

NEAR RIGHT: Resplendent in silk saris and gold jewellery, young women welcome guests to a Hindu wedding. FAR RIGHT: Indian dancers garbed in traditional costumes for the Chingay Parade during the Lunar New Year. Indians remain one of the islands most vibrant ethnic groups, determined to retain the rich vestiges of their past. Children are sent for music and dance lessons from an early age, later performing in festivals as part of various Indian cultural groups.

in Singapore when they had completed their sentences.

The proximity of the Indian prison settlements is one reason why Serangoon Road came to be characterised as "Little India". As other Indians arrived to provide cheap labour for municipal works, they too settled in quarters close to Serangoon Road. Another factor which drew them to that area was the ample grass and water in the adjacent swamplands, making it popular with those Indians who had boldly invested in cattle.

It wasn't until the boom time of the 1920s,

LEFT: Goldsmith shop in Little India. ABOVE: Silk store along Serangoon Road. Indians were among the first immigrants to the new crown colony of Singapore, mostly merchants who saw the golden opportunities of a new free-trade port on the Straits of Malacca.

when wives and children began arriving from India, that Serangoon Road evolved into a proper residential community. Building on family contacts, people moved in as cattle moved out. The commercial potential of the area grew as tradesmen and service folk began providing more amenities for households. Although there are more Chinese living there than Indians, the precinct remains distinctively Indian because of its concentration of Indians.

At any time of the day, to walk down Serangoon Road is to encounter the pungent aroma of various spices being ground in a quaint (but noisy) mill; to discover a sudden conformity of skin colour, yet spread across a range of hues from North Indian fair to South Indian chocolate; to espy a moustache on almost every man and a traditional sari on every other woman. The cacophony of noises has a sublevel of vibrant business deals, of kin and kith being encountered and re-encountered, of constant traffic abrading the metalled road. Every variation of that simplified term, an Indian, comes to Serangoon Road sooner or later. It is the palpable heart of Indianness in Singapore.

Most of the Indians in Singapore today are Tamils, originally from the southeastern state of Tamil Nadu. They make up two-thirds of the community. The great majority of the Tamils are Hindus, but a significant proportion are Muslim, who are especially prominent as small businessmen. The Muslim-Indians predominate in the "five-and-ten cent" convenience stores located on the ground floor of selected Housing Development Board (HDB) apartment blocks. However, some of the most successful Indian businessmen also hail from this tightly knit Muslim community. Few Hindu Tamils opt for a career in business, most of them preferring to aspire to the professions. Indeed the Hindu Tamils are prominent as lawyers, doctors and teachers, and also in less-skilled occupations such as dockyard workers and clerical jobs. Many can also be found in the civil service.

Another distinct subgroup are the Malayalees — Indians from the southwestern state of Kerala. They tend to be better educated (Kerala has long boasted more than 90 per cent literacy) and make up about eight per cent of the local Indian population.

The Indians remain one of Singapore's most culturally vibrant groups. Several Indian cultural groups thrive on the patronage of parents who send their children for a musical and dance grounding from an early age. But at the same time, in the larger community, there is an erosion of ethnic language skills and, some say, the sense of tradition as well, as young Indian children concentrate on English. They shun their mother tongues, from which they derive meagre economic value and increasingly little social advantage.

The community is, in the view of some, also going through a critical period of adjustment as its historical advantage of a strong command of the English language is eroded by a widespread English education for all of Singapore's ethnic groups and increasing competition for civil service employment. But the Indian community is reacting with a sense of self-help, turning to its educated elite and social workers to devise education programmes to help the next generation. Indeed, it's this perception of crisis that is engendering for the first time a sense of unity among the disparate groups.

Indian provisions shop. All
the riches of the subcontinent are for sale in the shops
of Little India and Serangoon
Road — curry powders and
silk saris, flower garlands and
filigree gold jewellery, betel
nut and brass utensils.

CHAPTER FIVE

ONE MAN'S DREAM

This early print shows coolies moving cargo along the Singapore waterfront. The colony was founded in 1819 after Sir Stamford Raffles struck a deal with local Malay rulers. Although the island was little more than worthless swamp and jungle at that time, Raffles strategy was clear: to establish a British trading port that would break Dutch hegemony over the Straits of the Malacca. The notion succeeded beyond his wildest imagination.

Singapore has seen a lot of history in its 170 plus years, relatively short as national lifespans go. The city has been carved out of virgin jungle and swamp, fashioned into a bustling port through the blood, sweat and tears of thousands of people. The island has undergone various waves of immigration, a mingling of Malays, Chinese, Indians and Europeans.

But it can rightfully be said that early Singapore wouldn't have thrived if not for the astonishing vision of a certain man — Sir Stamford Raffles — who first set foot on the island in 1819 to claim it for the British crown. Yet Raffles was not your typical imperialist, for part of his dream was the development of a multiracial society that would work in concert to create the great entrepreneurial gateway.

In turn, Raffles' fraternal vision became the very cornerstone of 19th-century Singapore society; his dream became the dream of the hundreds of thousands who followed in his footsteps.

As the early illustrations and photographs in this chapter show, they strived together to create a magnificent harbour and a beautiful city, for the overall success of Singapore meant better lives for them all. By the turn of the 20th century, Singapore and its people had achieved their goal of becoming one of the world's great ports.

V. Adam lith.

ABOVE: A rare hand-coloured wood engraving showing the Jamae Mosque and Sri Mariamman Temple on South Bridge Road, respective places of Muslim and Hindu worship in what is now the Chinatown section of central Singapore. Although Raffles subdivided his young city into separate quarters for the various ethnic groups, some mingling was bound to ensue. LEFT: Traditional dress of an early 19th-century Malay inhabitant.

ABOVE: The early colonial waterfront of Singapore is barely recognizable from the high-rise profile that exists today. Chinese junks and smaller Malay *prahus* were the order of the day, although British clipper ships would soon rule the local waves. In the background is Fort Canning Hill, with Raffles' residence perched on the crest. RIGHT: Traditional dress of early 19th-century Chinese immigrants.

Opium den in early Chinatown. Life for the initial Chinese immigrants — called *sinkhek* or "new men" — was anything but easy. Most of them worked long hours as coolies on the wharves, returning after dark to dingy rooms they shared with dozens of other men. The mortality rate was high, their quarters were called "nurseries of disease" and they had little spare cash because they sent most it home. Yet they kept arriving, drawn by the prospect of a better life than in crowded China. Their universal dream was to retire back to their home villages as wealthy men. Few of them made it. ABOVE RIGHT: Late into the night, coolies struggle under the weight of coal bound for ships in the harbour. One of Singapore's major functions was as a refueling station for nautical traffic between the Far East and India. More than 3,000 vessels tied up in the colony's first three years, as the free port became a raging success. By the turn of the 20th century, Singapore was the world's seventh largest port. RIGHT: There were occasional tragedies, like the explosion that wrecked this iron paddle-steamer.

ABOVE: Although it's now crowded by other buildings, there was a time when the Thian Hock Keng Temple stood on open land along the waterfront. It was constructed in 1841, and was the first of Singapore's great Chinese temples. LEFT: Bengali coffee sellers. Like other immigrant groups, the Indians came with hopes of a better life, perhaps even riches. The first came with Raffles from Penang, but later waves hailed mostly from the south Indian state of Tamil Nadu. RIGHT: Malay *prahus* ready for the start of a New Year's Day regatta.

LEFT: **Lively scene along the late 19th-century waterfront, dubbed "A Singapore Crowd" by the photographer.**
ABOVE: **British officers and Indian sepoy troops manned the garrison at Singapore.**
RIGHT: **English society quickly came to the island in the form of Victorian dress, afternoon tea and posh bungalow dwellings.**

(32) Raffles Hotel, Singapore.

ABOVE: Raffles Hotel opened its doors in 1887, the brainchild of the Sarkies brothers, two Armenian immigrants. At once it became the focus of European life in the colony. Locals flocked here for afternoon tea on the terrace, sundowners at the Long Bar or flamboyant social functions in the ballroom. But Raffles was even more famous as a home-away-from-home for visiting scribes like Rudyard Kipling, Somerset Maugham and Joseph Conrad. LEFT: Portrait of "Shanghai Lily" above the Long Bar at Raffles.

BELOW: As a respite from the rigours of life in the tropics, Europeans gather for a drink at Raffles. BOTTOM : Rickshaw boys and Indian doormen were familiar sights in Raffles' circular driveway. BELOW LEFT: Postcard showing the full extent of Raffles, at the corner of Bras Basah and Beach Roads.

CHAPTER SIX

A TOUCH OF THE RAJ

WRITTEN BY GRETCHEN LIU

The Supreme Court faces onto the Padang. Finished in 1939 on the site of the old Hotel de l'Europe, the neo-classical structure was the last great statement of British colonial architecture in the colony. The Corinthian columns and interior murals are the work of Italian artist Cavaliere Rodolfo Nolli, but the overall design is credited to British government architect F. Dorrington Ward.

At its apogee around the turn of the century, the British ruled a quarter of the world's population and nearly a quarter of its land surface. Singapore was one of the jewels in the crown, a verdant isle in the Straits of Malacca strategically placed at the crossroads of trade between East and West and populated with immigrants in search of a better life.

Today the British Empire is an ever-distant memory. Singapore has enjoyed self-rule for 30 years, the last 25 as an independent nation. The descendants of those rugged immigrants now call themselves Singaporeans. And to continued importance as a seaport has been added an equally significant role in air travel.

The parting of ways in the 1950s was inevitable, for the myth of British superiority was shattered by World War II and the Japanese Occupation of Singapore. The empire that the sun never set on was already fast disappearing. Yet, all things considered, the parting was reasonably amicable. The British maintained a military presence here until the early 1970s, finally withdrawing because of the crippling expense of sustaining themselves as a world power.

While a new nation can appear at the stroke of midnight, the vestiges of the colonial past — languages, religions, manners, customs, conventions, systems of laws and the like — cannot simply disappcar overnight. Some are quietly abandoned, others discarded purposefully, still others clung to tenaciously. More commonly, perhaps, the bits and pieces of the colonial past are sensibly absorbed or modified over time to suit new needs. Singaporeans are, above all, a pragmatic people.

The most potent legacy of Empire in Singapore remains the English language, one of the four official tongues along with Malay, Tamil and Mandarin. English is the main language of instruction in schools, themselves part of a British modelled educa-

RIGHT: **Wee Chong Jin, former Chief Justice of the Singapore Supreme Court. Besides the traditional wig and gown, the British endowed the island republic with its legal system.** TOP: **The inner sanctum of the House of Parliament. This is the island's oldest surviving colonial structure, built as a private house in 1827 by Irish architect George Coleman, later used as a court house and then the colonial** **Legislative Assembly before becoming the home of Singapore's new Parliament in 1965.** ABOVE: **The Surrender Chamber on Sentosa Island charts the course of Singapore's demise and eventual liberation from Japanese Occupation. Shown here is Lord Louis Mountbatten, Supreme Commander of Allied Forces in Southeast Asia, accepting the Japanese surrender at City Hall in 1945.**

tion system that marries bilingualism and Asian values with exams set at high school by the Cambridge syndicate. Some wealthy Singaporeans still send their children to English boarding schools, while an Oxford or Cambridge degree continues to carry a certain added prestige, even though more young scholars now turn to the United States for their tertiary education. Visitors are often surprised to find how widely — and well — English is spoken in this Asian city-state. But while crisp voices read the evening news in Queen's English, in the streets a distinctly different

LEFT: **Whites and wickets on the Padang as Sunday sportsmen vie for glory at the Singapore Cricket Club, established in the 1840s for the distraction of homesick Englishmen.** RIGHT: **Ruggers rough it up in front of the City Hall, on the grounds of the old Singapore Recreation Club (1883).** BELOW: **Fierce competition for the Rolex Gold Cup at the Polo Club, another vestige of the colonial past.**

version of the language may be heard — "Singlish" as it's now called. This version, also known as Singapore English, crosses socio-economic barriers. Many Singaporeans, including the Oxford educated, can tailor their English to suit the company and the occasion, switching accents as easily as a pair of socks. Peppered with idiomatic phrases and Asian words, it has even begun to make its appearance in the works of young playwrights, novelists and song writers.

In the realm of government and the law, the English example is also evident. The democratically elected government is headed by a prime minister with an appointed ceremonial head of state, the president. The president's official residence, the Istana, was built in the 1860s to house the British colonial governor. Parliament is housed in Singapore's oldest colonial structure, an 1827 Palladian villa built for an English merchant on the north bank of the Singapore River.

Across the road from Parliament House is the High Court, an impressive neo-classical building from the 1930s. Here, Singapore barristers plead their cases in robes and wigs before judges who are themselves dressed like their English counterparts. The similarities go deeper than appearance, for Singapore's legal system is in most ways akin to that used in England.

In the realm of manners, customs and conventions, the colonial past lives on, often with great charm, even quaintness, alongside the recent invasion of fast-food restaurants, pop music and other aspects of American youth culture. Sunday services

LEFT: Lingering memories of Empire persist, as witnessed in this hood ornament on a car used to transport guests to the Kranji War Memorial for a visit by the Duke of Kent. RIGHT: From double-decker buses to trishaws, Singapore also owes much of its transportation flavour to British influence. BELOW: The polished brass buckle and crisp white uniform of a Presidential Guard at the Istana palace. The British bequeathed Singapore with a passion for splendid uniforms, as seen in the contemporary dress of both the police and the armed forces.

at St. Andrew's cathedral, or one of the other 19th-century Anglican churches. A leisurely afternoon tea with cucumber sandwiches and scones. Midday curry tiffin. A Saturday or Sunday at the races. Watching ponies at the Polo Club. Whiskey stengahs at sundown in the Cricket Club and cricket on the adjacent Padang, the green sward in the heart of the city. Gin slings at the Long Bar of the fabled Raffles Hotel. Bridge and tennis at the Tanglin Club, which now admits Asians but retains its slightly snooty British character. Turkey and Christmas pudding in December.

Perhaps the most visible reminders of Singapore's colonial past, and those most easily accessible to visitors, are to be found in the streets and buildings of the city itself. Singapore, like many of the other great British colonial cities — Bombay, Calcutta, Hong Kong, Sydney or Shanghai — was built where virtually nothing existed before. At its founding in 1819, it was largely the creation of one individual, Thomas Stamford Raffles. Against a backdrop of tense

English-Dutch relations in the Far East in the wake of the Napoleonic Wars and restrictive Dutch trade policies, this brash young officer of the British East India Company went in search of a place the British could call their own in the Malacca Straits.

Raffles himself never spent much time in Singapore, just three short visits between 1819 and 1823 adding up to ten months. But he had a vision — and the determination to impose it. Arriving in late 1822 after a three year absence, Raffles found urban chaos quite different from the tidy town he

envisaged. He set to work immediately drafting a Town Plan and appointing a committee to oversee its implementation. By the time he left Singapore for good, nine months later, he was satisfied with his efforts.

This city plan is still in evidence today. It lives on in the Civic and Cultural District, in the ethnic neighbourhoods of Chinatown and Kampong Glam, and in street names as well. Walk the older downtown streets of this tropical isle and you will discover for yourself that the colonial past coexists easily with the present.

At the heart of the original settlement, Raffles allocated land for government use on the north

bank of the Singapore River and plots for a commercial district on the south bank. Today the north bank is the heart of the Civic and Cultural District, one of a dozen Conservation Areas designated in 1989. The colonial buildings here span more than a century, from roughly 1830 to 1930. These were truly the foundation stones of the Empire.

Near to the river are Parliament House, Victoria Concert Hall and Theatre and the Empress Place Building, recently renovated as an exhibition venue. Beyond are the Supreme Court, the old City Hall, the Cricket Club and St. Andrew's Cathedral. Anchoring this ensemble is the Padang, an emerald rectangle that once flanked the seafront but that is now landlocked by a kilometre or more. Not far away is the National Museum, another 19th-century treas-

LEFT: Traditional shophouses like these in the Tanjong Pagar Restoration Area are not so much a British creation as the synthesis of several architectural styles brought together by colonial rule in the East. They combine Indian, Malay and Chinese design, but somehow wouldn't look out of place in Bristol or Brighton. RIGHT: Empress Place is the crowning glory of colonial architecture on the island. Built in the 1860s as a court house, the building later hosted the Immigration Department and other government offices before undergoing a $25-million restoration and reopening as a museum and exhibition space for Chinese relics in 1989.

ure, nestled against Fort Canning Hill.

While the Civic District has survived relatively intact, little survives of the original Commercial Square. The quad itself, fashioned in the 1820s from a hillock, is now an urban park. Underneath is a large subway station. Appropriately renamed Raffles Place decades ago, the square is now enveloped in steel and glass — skyscrapers that symbolize Singapore's progress since independence.

That none of the colonial buildings have survived is not surprising. To maintain itself, a city must have an economic raison d'etre. Singapore's very soul has always been tied to mercantile expansion, so even a century ago new commercial buildings rarely lasted more than a few decades.

Most of Singapore's early churches, schools, commercial and public buildings were the efforts of

LEFT: The magnificent copula of the National Museum. It started life in 1887 as a place to display Sir Stamford Raffles' natural history and anthropology collections. Nowadays, the museum specializes in the art, history and culture of Asia. Many of the nation's treasures are protected within its sturdy walls, including the priceless Haw Par jade collection.

ABOVE AND RIGHT: Telok Ayer Market is one of Singapore's latest renovation schemes. The extraordinary cast-iron structure was made in Scotland, transported by ship in hundreds of pieces and then erected on the Singapore waterfront in 1894 for use as a food market. For restoration, the structure was disassembled, then erected again in 1989.

anonymous builders and craftsmen, along with a handful of military and civil engineers, surveyors, priests, merchants and other architectural amateurs. A notable exception was George Drumgold Coleman, an Irishman who made Singapore his home from 1827 until the early 1840s as architect, surveyor, contractor, Superintendent of Public Works and Overseer of Convicts. His skill is evident in the Armenian Church (1835) and the Caldwell House (1840). He also designed Parliament House, although the structure has been renovated many times and bears little trace of its original Palladian symmetry. Coleman's other masterpieces exist only in faded

photographs. Even then, their intrinsic beauty is readily apparent. Each bore classical proportions and symmetry, and sensitivity to the tropics — with deep verandahs, high ceilings, overhanging roofs for shade, an open floor plan and louvered windows which gave light yet reduced glare — high standards that were happily followed by others.

In Raffles scheme, the various ethnic communities each had their own *kampung,* or village. The Chinese, who Raffles knew would always comprise the largest group, were given the area south of the river beyond Boat Quay and Commercial Square — today's Chinatown. The Indians (Chulias) were moved upstream on the same side of the river, to the area where Chulia and Market streets are today. Europeans and wealthy Asians were relocated to land just beyond the government area where Beach Road and North Bridge Road were laid out. Beyond, in Kampong Glam, the followers of Sultan Hussein were given property and Arabs, Bugis, Javanese and other Muslims encouraged to settle.

Singapore's third important ethnic enclave, Little India, has an altogether different history. It grew spontaneously over time. All three still thrive and are popular both with visitors and locals as clusters of good food, bargains and old-time ambience. The streets are still lined with two and three-storey shophouses with elegant plasterwork on their facades. Shophouses also hark back to Singapore's early days when such structures — in a liner arrangement with specified widths and linked by a covered walkway — were introduced "for the sake of regularity and conformity."

A city at its inception can be the folly of one free-minded individual, but Sir Stamford ensured a dynamic towards order and cohesion within the framework of urban Singapore. In those early years, Singapore's status as a free port, its relative uniformity and convenient location set the stage for the great drama of design that has unfolded in the decades since. The opening of the Suez Canal in the 1860s, tin mining in Malaya and the production of rubber in the early years of this century, and the economic boom of the last three decades are some of significant factors which have affected the urban landscape and determined the various buildings constructed over time.

Singapore never completely turned her back on the colonial past. But like many new nations, it has taken some time to sort out what to discard and what to keep.

ABOVE: **Raffles Hotel, the most enduring symbol of British colonial rule in the East, completed its own massive renovation in early 1991. Behind it towers the** massive Raffles City complex, emblematic of post-colonial Singapore and its high-tech profile. LEFT: Colonial-style bungalows such as this once housed British civil servants and senior military personnel. With independence in 1965, they were sold to the new Singapore government at a bargain price. After years of neglect in favour of modern condos, the bungalows are now among the hottest residential properties on the island, as Singaporeans rediscover their colonial heritage.

CHAPTER SEVEN

A WALK ON THE WILD SIDE

Written By Joe Yogerst

Bukit Timah Nature Reserve, now part of the fledgling Singapore National Park system, preserves the island's last tract of primary rainforest, as well as it's highest point, a 162-metre hill of the same name. Among the reserve's inhabitants are troupes of long-tailed macaque monkeys, diminutive and shy mousedeer, pangolin anteaters, flying lemurs, tropical squirrels and deadly snakes such as the king cobra. Tropical hardwoods tower more than 50 metres here.

 My Singapore experience is much different than your average person, be they a resident or visitor. I live in a low density area near the centre of the island, surrounded by lush tropical vegetation and various animals that have made this island their home since the dawn of time.

I can't see a high-rise building, nor can I hear the buzz of traffic so familiar in much of Singapore. There's a papaya tree outside my bedroom window, and I awake most mornings to the sound of birds. The evening silence is broken by the drone of cicada bugs, or the croaking of the gecko lizards that dart up and down my living room walls. I know there are sizeable bullfrogs in the garden, and somewhere out there in the shadows lurk pythons.

Just down the road is the Bukit Timah Nature Reserve, where I was once confronted by a troupe of long-tailed macaques who determined not to let me pass. Flying lemurs, pangolins and tiny mousedeer still live among the trees and undergrowth. From the crest of Bukit Timah hill — the highest point in Singapore — I can gaze out across the massive undeveloped heart of the island, a primeval panorama of misty rainforest and blue-grey lakes. You can walk for hours through this vast water catchment area without seeing another human being or coming upon any sort of man-made structure.

I moved to Singapore for a tropical island experience, but until I began to explore it's various nooks and crannies, I never released how close to nature you can still venture in this futuristic city-state. Only a third of the republic is given over to forest, parks and gardens, but it's enough to get lost in.

Take the outlying islands as an example. There are 57 of them, mostly in the Straits of Malacca but with a few scattered in the Johor Strait between Singapore and Malaysia. Some have been converted to "blue collar" islands with petro-chemical plants, container terminals and military bases. But most of them are still relatively undeveloped and unexplored — even by native Singaporeans.

Pulau Ubin has the roughest edge, a real

LEFT: One of the more curious episodes of Singapore's natural history lore was the case of three elephants who swam several kilometres across the Johor Strait and took up residence on Pulau Tekong island in 1990. They were quickly removed by the Malaysian Elephant Translocation Unit in a joint operation with the zoo and armed forces. **RIGHT:** Ah Meng greets visitors on the Orangutan Terrace at the Singapore Zoological Gardens. One of the world's best zoos, it specializes in rare and endangered Southeast Asian animals such as the orangutan.

rogue of an island. It was once dominated by a vast rubber estate and deep stone quarries, but the plantation was abandoned and granite is no longer in such demand. Meanwhile, nature has taken over again with a vengeance. The mixed forest that now covers much of Ubin is a perfect habitat for monitor lizards, snakes, flying foxes and thousands of tropical birds. In fact, the island is said to have more avian species than Taman Negara, Malaysia's huge rainforest park.

In keeping with its rustic image, there are several distinctly rugged ways to explore Ubin. You can hire an old, beat-up taxi from near the ferry pier for a rough and tumble journey along Ubin's unpaved roads. You can set off on foot along those same dirt tracks, and you can also survey the landscape by mountain bike or kayak — the circumnavigation takes about a full day. If you're really adventurous, try a

course at the island's Outward Bound school. There are several tasty seafood restaurants on the "back side" of Ubin. And if you happen to visit during festival time, try to catch a *wayang* performance at the municipal stage in Ubin village.

On the ferry from Changi Point to Ubin, you can spot the rugged green outline of Pulau Tekong on the eastern skyline. The island is off limits to the public now because it's a jungle training ground for the Singapore Armed Forces (SAF). But not long ago it was the venue for one of Singapore's more endearing wildlife sagas.

Three elephants swam two kilometres across the Johor Straits and took up residence on Tekong. No one knows what prompted them to leave their Malaysian jungle home: perhaps they were scared away by loggers or poachers. But they took an immediate liking to Tekong, with its expansive rainforest and multitude of munchy plants. The military didn't view the situation in a similar light. The big creatures might be injured during army operations, they moaned. But secretly it was whispered that the generals were more fearful of the recruits getting stomped on in an elephant stampede.

Despite public sentiment that favoured leaving the elephants alone, a huge military-like operation was mounted to capture the misguided beasts. The Malaysian Elephant Relocation Unit, in league

ABOVE: Singapore's parks and gardens take on many forms, like the immaculately landscaped Chinese Garden with its Sung Dynasty-style pagodas and a 65-metre ornamental bridge. LEFT: Fort Canning Park is another new member of the national park system. Remains of a 600-year-old Malay settlement have been found on the hill, once sacred to local people. Raffles chose Canning for his private bungalow, which later became the first Governor's House, and as the site of an experimental tropical nursery which evolved into the Botanic Gardens. RIGHT: A trishaw driver takes it easy amid the cool and quiet of a Singapore park.

Founded in 1859 on its present site, the Botanic Gardens are one of Singapore's most popular attractions, both for locals and visitors. It was here in 1877 that botanist Henry "Mad" Ridley planted rubber seedlings that had been smuggled from Brazil via Kew Gardens and Ceylon. His successful experiment led to the Malayan rubber industry. The gardens displays more than 2,500 varieties of plants and flowers, including Singapore's national bloom, the Vanda Miss Joaquim orchid (left).

with the Singapore Zoo, darted and abducted the elephants, whisking them away by truck to new homes in a Malaysian forest reserve.

Nature of a different breed can be experienced on a cruise to the Southern Islands — Kusu, Lazarus, St John's and the Sisters — which lie astride the ship-strewn Straits of Malacca. These tiny islands boast Singapore's best beaches, while St Johns and Lazarus also support good sized chunks of tropical forest. Kusu and St John's can be reached by regular ferry from Jardine Steps. But my favourite way to explore the Southern group is to pack an ice chest with drinks, hire a bumboat from Clifford Pier and chart a beach-hopping course between islands.

With many of its social and economic goals achieved, the Singapore government has jumped on the environmental bandwagon as part of its con-

ABOVE: South American macaw parrots at the Jurong Bird Park. With over 3,000 birds and the world's largest walk-in aviary, the park is a paradise for bird watchers. Of particular note are the Southeast Asian species and a night house that displays rarely seen nocturnal birds. UPPER LEFT: Plunging into the Jurong aviary is a 30-metre artificial waterfall. LEFT: Parrots and peacocks can also be seen on Sentosa Island, while graceful fan palms are rather ubiquitous around town.

certed effort to improve the overall quality of life in the republic. For instance, in early 1990, $75 million was applied to the formation of a National Parks Board to administer and upgrade three nature areas: Bukit Timah, Fort Canning and the Botanical Gardens.

Bukit Timah is the grandfather of the island's nature reserves, set aside in 1883 as a patch of pristine rainforest and significant today because it's the only Singapore forest that has never been logged. Beneath a canopy of towering trees, the jungle trails are dark at midday. Some of the giant hardwoods reach 50 metres in height, with rattan vines suspended from the branches and epiphytic ferns clutching at the trunks for support. Down at ground level are fungus, ferns and bizarre "carnivorous" plants like the Monkey Cup, which can capture and digest insects in its leafy pitchers. From off in the distance come the sharp cracks of an army rifle range, reverberating off the hillsides, somehow adding to the atavistic ambience.

Several years ago the government developed a master plan for conservation with over 20 sites shortlisted for protection, most of them on the island's northern fringe. Sungei Buloh Nature Reserve is the most accessible of these areas, a sprawling "ecological park" near Kranji Dam that embraces many different natural habitats including mudflats, fishponds, coconut groves and one of the island's last mangrove swamps. Elevated walkways take visitors on a journey through Singapore's primordial past.

What Singapore hasn't been able to preserve, it has been able to recreate within the confines of the Botanic Gardens. The first such garden was founded in 1822 by Sir Stamford Raffles as an experimental plot for growing spices. It was re-established at its present location in Tanglin in 1859 and is now considered the leading botanic showcase of South East Asia. The orchid enclosure alone boasts 250 different hybrids or species including the giant Tiger orchid and Singapore's national flower, the Vanda Miss Joaquim orchid.

A number of plant oddities can be found around the gardens: the vegetable-hummingbird plant, South American cannonball tree, monkey pot trees, a sacred Buddhist plant called the Botree, and a 230-year-old cotton plant. Examples of famous tropical plant crops are also a speciality: cinnamon, clove and nutmeg from the Spice Islands; lumber industry heavyweights such as teak; food plants like durian, kola nut and oil palm. Perhaps the most famous plant of all is the Para Rubber Tree, a second-generation offspring of seedlings smuggled out of Brazil and planted in the gardens in 1877 by botanist Henry "Mad" Ridley. This experiment gave birth to the Malayan rubber industry. Soon to open is a new Botanic Gardens segment called the Cloud

Forest, a glass-enclosed mountainside that will house temperate climate plants of high altitude Malaysia and Indonesia. Visitors will be able to ascend the mountain by means of foot paths, walking through artificial clouds generated by a behind-the-scenes vaporizing machine. Other new projects including cacti, water and spice gardens that will expand the total size of the arboretum to 54 hectares.

In conjunction with its ambitious national park plans, Singapore is also in the midst of a massive "Garden of the Orient" scheme that will see the development of 300 additional hectares of parks and gardens — many of the plants chosen by Botanic

LEFT: **Orchid farm near Mandai. Although very few orchids are native to the island, commercial cultivation was pioneered in Singapore thanks to John Laycock who developed the first long-lasting exportable orchids that could reach Europe, Japan and America without dying. Fish farms and vegetable gardens can still be found on the northern fringes of the island. Hydroponics and other high-tech farming methods are the wave of the future, as science takes over from green thumbs.**

LEFT: Much of the centre of the island is given over to a huge catchment area that serves the dual functions of storing water and preserving vast tracts of forest and woodland. ABOVE: From the top of Bukit Timah hill, the catchment area resembles a dark and brooding primeval jungle. In fact, tigers stalked this forest until the 1940s. RIGHT: The forest floor in Bukit Timah Nature Reserve.

Gardens experts. These new green areas will include campgrounds and hiking trails, with the $500-million project set for completion by the year 2000.

Another leader in its field is the Singapore Zoological Gardens, one of the world's best wildlife facilities. The collection started life after the Second World War as a menagerie of cast-off British military pets. A proper zoo was established in 1973, and under the brilliant guidance of director Bernard Harrison it has grown into a comprehensive and well designed showcase. The zoo features animals from around the globe, but its forte is South East Asian fauna: orangutans, tapirs, sambar deer, tigers, hog deer, elephants, sun bear and various monkeys. Free form, natural enclosures are another distinct feature; especially noteworthy are the crocodile and polar bear exhibits, the Komodo dragon exhibit and the orangutan island, which has the world's largest breeding group of the endangered orange apes.

Beyond the zoological gardens, skirting the north and west coasts, are the last truly rural parts of Singapore. Along the rural lanes of places like Choa Chu Kang, Lim Chu Kang and Yishun one stumbles along the most unlikely Singapore scenes: a *kampung*-style wooden houses surrounded by a phalanx of towering coconut palms; tiny farms where vegetables, tropical fruits, pigs and poultry are raised; vast Chinese cemeteries with their characteristic womb-shaped tombs; and fragrant orchid plantations that export more than $10 million in blooms each year. At one time, there were over 2,000 pig farms too, but these are being gradually phased out because of their adverse effect on the rural environment.

But even these bucolic scenes are changing. Like much of the rest of Singapore, the future of the farmlands lies in science and technology. Land is growing more scarce by the day, which means that farmers must learn how to produce more from less soil. They will do this by applying white-collar management techniques to agriculture and using high-tech innovations such as hydroponics and biogenetics. Singapore's 21st-century farms may look the same from outside, but behind barn doors they'll be as super-efficient as the island's factories.

So from now on, when you imagine Singapore, don't simply think of the glittering skyline, infinite shopping and exotic food. For the island is also a great place to take a walk on the wild side of Asia.

CHAPTER EIGHT

A TASTE OF THE TROPICS

WRITTEN BY VIOLET OON

Is there a better place to eat on the planet? Singapore sustenance includes (clockwise from upper left) Chinese chicken rice, Malay satay with peanut sauce and Indian curry. Other culinary influences derive from Indonesia, Portugal and Britain.

If there's one thing that unites Singaporeans, it is their unbounded love for food and the ways it is eaten. Not just any food, but Singapore food. It's more than just fodder for the body. They luxuriate in the taste, texture, aroma, appearance and sound that food makes as it is sears in the wok or crunches in the mouth. The act of eating is also the golden opportunity to break bread with friends. Fellowship is very much what food is about in Singapore.

Just what is this food that inspires such devotion amongst Singaporeans? A devotion so intense that a fortnight away from the island evokes severe cases of withdrawal. Citizens have been known to head straight for Newton Circus, or any of the other late-night eateries, straight from Changi Airport, complete with luggage. As for Singaporeans who have to live abroad for long stretches of time, nearly all will say that what they miss most about home is the food.

Does it deserve this devotion? Quite frankly, yes. There is a unique combination of lip-smacking deliciousness, variety, very low prices and ultra-high quality that characterizes both the preparation and raw ingredients that make up Singapore cuisine. Is there really a typical dish? No. And is there one characteristic culture of this food? No, again. Yet every Singaporean knows just what you're talking

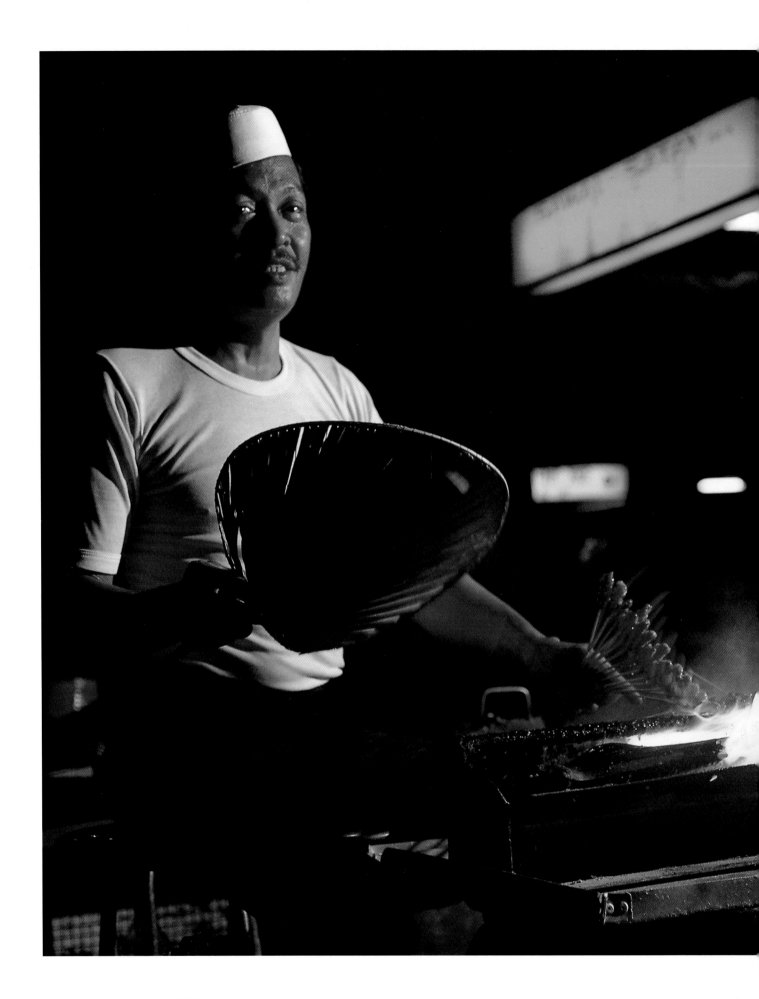

about when you mention Singaporean food.

Like a riot of colours and patterns in a painting that are contrasting and yet make up a cohesive whole, Singapore food is above all flamboyant. And few places capture this flamboyance as well as the much maligned Newton Circus, a massive outdoor food centre housing a wide variety and large number of food stalls. Tourist trap it may be, but seasoned critics from the food capitals of the world are immediately won over by "the very sense of life of the

LEFT: **The popular Satay Club opposite the Padang specializes in succulent roast meats on skewers, usually eaten with onions, cucumber and tangy peanut sauce.**
ABOVE: **Hokkien prawns and noodles fried in a wok at the fabled Newton Circus hawker centre. Outdoor food stalls are the paragon of Singapore dining, frequented by everyone from construction workers in sweaty overalls to businessmen in suit and tie.**

place," says Mimi Sheraton of *Conde Nast Traveler* magazine in New York.

Be forewarned: Newton Circus can be overwhelming, especially when giant tour buses disgorge camera-totting Japanese by the hundreds. They swarm the place and order huge platters full of giant prawns, crabs and lobsters. Package-tour Japanese, with the other tourists who pack the place nightly, have pushed prices sky high. Personally, I enjoy eating breakfast at Newton Circus, where I can enjoy a bowl of *bak kut teh* (pork ribs tea) or *niang dou fu* under the shade of the giant angsana trees.

Unless you are with a local or you're good at bargaining prices, avoid the seafood stalls. You can find much better meals at lower prices elsewhere in Singapore. More about this later. But first, back to Newton. The wise diner — the best time for eating is 6pm to midnight — should choose one dish from a number of different stalls. I would suggest chicken rice, fried Hokkien *mee, rojak*, a Malay rice dish called *nasi padang*, Indian *mee goreng, satay*, roast duck rice and a Malay dessert called *putu piring*. The list goes on. Prices are listed on a board above the front of the stalls; they average a few Singapore dollars each.

My other favourite hawker food centre is Bugis Square in Lavender Street. This is also brightly

Red chillies on sale at the Geylang Serai Market. Spicy heat is a familiar characteristic of Malay and Indonesian food, as well as indigenous Nonya cuisine. Yet chillies should never overwhelm the subtle flavour of the other spices.

lit and raucously noisy. Well heeled Singaporeans dine and sup here; you can hardly spy a foreign face. Since Bugis is privately owned and operated, the quality is better than at Newton. The barbecued chicken wings, claypot rice, the famous chicken rice from the original Bugis Street, and barbecued seafoods on banana leaves are all excellent. There's also a *dian xin* (dim sum) stall here.

For more discriminating gourmets longing for old fashioned tastes, the food centre in a court-yard — Lim Liak Street in Tiong Bahru — is the place. It's not visible from the road because stalls

Of all the tropical fruits available in Singapore, the most loved — and hated — is the durian. The controversy here lies in the durian's potent flavour and pungent aroma. Considered a smelly nuisance, they are banned from the MRT and airline flights.

face inward to the courtyard.

At night, Hwa Yuen Porridge serves one of the last authentic versions of *congee* (Cantonese rice porridge) left in Singapore. Those in the know usually order a bowlful of smooth-as-silk porridge and a plateful of *yu sheng* (raw fish), wolf herring cut into paper-thin slivers. A sprinkling of light soya sauce, cooked peanut oil, julienne of spring onions and a hint of sliced chillies will garnish the fish. With your chopsticks, you take a slice of the fish, dip it into the hot porridge and then let it half-cook before eating. The *bao* at this centre is also well known, along with the Teochew *chai chwee pow* sold by the Eur family at Lean Huat, stall number 11-N.

One food centre that you shouldn't miss is Ellenborough Market in New Bridge Road, opposite Carpenter Street. The third story houses some of the best of traditional Teochew cooking in Singapore. Tycoons, *tai tais* (rich housewives) and simple folk eat elbow-to-elbow in this historical repository of Teochew culinary expertise. Besides hawker stalls serving one-dish meals in the best street tradition, Ellenborough also boasts excellent Teochew restaurant cooking.

I would also have a meal at any of the fully fledged Teochew restaurants at Ellenborough. The raw ingredients — a wide variety of fish, prawns and vegetables — are laid out in glass-fronted refrigerators. The waiter will tell you what's fresh for the day. Among recommended dishes are braised goose in

LEFT: A Nonya chef grinds chillies in a stone mortar. Nonya or Peranakan cuisine is an invention of the Straits Chinese, early immigrants to the Malay Peninsula who combined Chinese style with local ingredients. RIGHT: Nonya dishes at a restaurant in Peranakan Place. BELOW: A popular Nonya dessert called *ang koo kueh*.

soya sauce, deep-fried Chinese pate rolls called *ngoh hiang* and chicken fried in chestnuts. On no account should you miss the steamed Teochew-style pomfret. A meal for four should cost about S$60. The best hours are from 8am to 2pm.

If you're not in the know, food centres — or hawker centres as they are also called — are outdoor or indoor eating hubs which house a large number of food stalls, each serving a particular dish or set of dishes. They literally offer the world on a table top. Chinese, Malay, Indian and hints of English cooking can be found in these centres. You can place your orders at any stall and sit at any table you want to. Hawker food in Asia is street cuisine. Traditionally the food was sold out of carts pushed around a particular area. Both dishes and style of cooking are unique, found neither at home nor in restaurants.

Some gourmets prefer to confine their meals to food centres. But avoid this, as you will miss out on a lot. For instance, *kopi tiams* (coffee shops) and medium priced restaurants have a lot to offer. Several areas come to mind.

For an intimate taste of India, head for Serangoon Road and its labyrinth of side streets. Campbell Street, Cuff Road, Buffalo Road and Race Course Road comprise the core of Little India, where the culture of the sub-continent has been transported lock, stock and barrel to Singapore. The omni-present Tamil songs, the sweet scent of jasmine and the pungency of cardamon and cloves, the flow of the saris, provide a special sense of place.

Race Course Road is a sort of curry lane and the particular style of food on offer here is southern,

LEFT: An old cafe in Chinatown with typical Peranakan floor tiles and wooden furniture. Food ranges through Cantonese, Hokkien, Teochew and Szechaun. RIGHT: Chinese-style tea has never lost its appeal among local residents. A good place to learn about and witness the traditional Chinese tea ceremony is the Tea Chapter on Neil Road in the Tanjong Pagar district.

spicy, fiery and eaten off banana leaves. Each house has as its speciality, costing S$14–$22. Banana Leaf Apolo and Muthu's Curry are the most famous restaurants, but I also enjoy the curries at Our Makan Shop.

If you're really adventurous, head into the suburbs, where Thasevi Food at 237 Jalan Kayu serves what is believed to be the best *roti prata* in Singapore. This fluffy Indian bread-cum-pancake is eaten with a variety of curries and is available from 6am to 11pm.

Nonya food — that happy marriage of Chinese and Malay cuisine — is a taste experience that should never be missed in Singapore. The Nonya and Baba Restaurant in River Valley Road serves a fair version of the cuisine. But those who want a true insight into Straits Chinese culture should head east to Katong, one of the oldest middle-class suburbs of

Singapore, where the shophouses of East Coast Road boast an exciting array of foods. Near Chapel Road are a few restaurants serving Nonya food, as well as a range of Hainanese dishes. For a taste of Nonya cakes and pastries, any of the Bengawan Solo cake shop branches around town will meet your needs.

Singapore has always been known as a crossroads of East and West, offering the best of both worlds. Nowhere is this more evident than in the elegant restaurants that are so abundantly found in the city. Note that in Singapore, most of the best restaurants are found in hotels — that's because we like to make grand entrances.

Nouvelle Chinese cuisine — exquisite touches of finesse in combination with superb service and restrained decor — is best found at restau-

LEFT: **Seafood seller at Geylang Serai Market.** BELOW: **Mr Lee's Chinese fish stall at Zhujiao wet market in Little India.** RIGHT: **Steamed lobster at Newton Circus. Fishy business is good business when it comes to Singapore food. Chinese seafood relies on a fresh catch, the fish and shellfish kept alive in tanks until the last possible moment. Meanwhile, dried fish like *ikan bilis* is a staple of Malay cuisine.**

rants like Chang Jiang (Goodwood Park Hotel), Ruyi (Hyatt Regency Hotel), Cherry Garden (Oriental Hotel), Li Bai (Sheraton Towers Hotel) and Lei Garden. In recent years, Japanese food has gained a wide following. One of the island's more interesting Japanese eating events is Keyaki, at the Pan Pacific Hotel, a traditional Japanese lodge on the roof garden which offers *teppanyaki, sushi* and *sashimi* among a wide range of Japanese dishes.

Also pay a visit to Tanjong Pagar, the historical district, where 13 restaurants and drinks outlets have sprung up since restoration was finished. Among the cuisines represented are Korean (Haebok), Chinese seafood, Italian (Da Paolo) and Padang (Pagi). Every room has a view. But for that spectacular panorama, two restaurants come to mind — the Pinnacle at OUB Centre in Raffles Place serving a combination of exquisite Cantonese and French cooking; while the Compass Rose in the Westin Stamford Hotel serves fine European cooking with an Asian touch. There's a food experience in Singapore to suit every mood, pocket and taste. Try it. You'll like it.

Sometimes the simplest food is the best: a Chinese woman sells bananas from a pavement stall off Serangoon Road. Singapore is an entrepôt for fresh fruit from around the world. Besides Asian delicacies, markets also display Canadian apples, Central American bananas, California oranges and New Zealand kiwi fruit.

CHAPTER NINE

HOLLYWOOD EAST

Written By Joe Yogerst

Bright lights, big city: the big banks of the financial district cast their glimmering profile over the restaurants and bars of Boat Quay. Singapore may not be the most exciting nightlife town in Asia, but like everything else in life it's trying hard to catch up. With the same enthusiasm shown earlier on economic and educational progress, Singaporeans are now trying to add a little cultural "soul" to their city.

Seventy thousand people gather on a sweltering night beneath the arc lamps of a giant stadium, braving the heat and humidity for hours, waiting for the show to begin. Finally the lights go down, dark forms take the stage and the crowd goes wild as Michael Jackson dances into the spotlight. This would be no great shakes in Pittsburgh or Paris, where stadium rock is par for the course. But this is Singapore. And it's a *very* big deal. Not just for young people, but the nation as a whole. Because the country's sudden ability to attract mammoth stars is just one more sign that Singapore is coming of age, this time in the world of entertainment.

Singapore is attracting all kinds of big-time acts these days. Music legends like Eric Clapton, Bob Dylan, Deep Purple and Ray Charles. Cutting edge groups like Metallica, INXS, Bobby Brown and Color Me Badd. Even the triple crown of the opera world: Luciano Pavarotti, Jose Carreras and Placido Domingo. But that's not all. Singapore is also luring major West End and Broadway stage productions — *Evita, My Fair Lady* and *Phantom of the Opera.*

Why are all of these acts suddenly coming to Singapore? Because the island's increasingly well versed and sophisticated audiences are giving these people the kind of treatment they expect from American and European audiences but that has tradition-

If Singapore has an equivalent of Times Square, it has to be the intersection of Orchard and Scotts roads, in the shadow of the pagoda-shaped Dynasty Hotel. Half a million young people gather for a giant street party called Singapore Swing on the eve of National Day (9th August). The rest of the year they party in the various karaoki bars, nightclubs, pubs, discos and open-air cafes along Orchard Road. There's no street quite like it in all Asia.

By daylight, Orchard Road takes on a much different flavour. In the minds of both locals and visitors, the street is synonymous with shopping. You can buy Chinese silks and Ming Dynasty antiques, haute couture from Paris and Milan, electronic gizmos from Tokyo and Taiwan, and American gourmet deli foods.

ally been rare in Asia. Canadian rocker Bryan Adams was shocked that so many people knew the words to his songs. He was even more surprised when the kids got up and danced through the show. In fact, nearly everyone is surprised by the local enthusiasm for culture and entertainment, whether it's a rock concert or classical concerto.

The cavalcade of concerts and plays fit perfectly into one of Singapore's latest goals: transforming the island into Hollywood East, the entertainment capital of the Orient. That title is currently held by Hong Kong, but local promoters figure that with 1997 breathing down the neck of creative expression in the British colony, Singapore is set to snatch the gold ring.

Singapore's Economic Development Board (EDB) is helping to boost the standard of local creativity with its customary infusion of enthusiasm and funding. In good technocratic fashion, it recently established a committee — the Creative Services Strategic Business Unit — to identify organize and foster areas of creative and entertainment growth. The EDB is also funding Singapore's own version of *Fame*: an Institute for Communicative Arts to generate technical expertise and artistic talent in the film, television, music and publishing industries.

But the major thrust is coming from the private sector. By investing in first-rate production facilities and working with experienced foreign talent and technicians, Singapore's entertainment gurus hope to mould the island into one of the major creative forces in Asia by the end of the decade. And not just English-language productions, but movies and music in Mandarin, Malay and Tamil too.

One of the first steps in that direction was the development of a homegrown movie studio in suburban Jurong, a sprawling compound called Tang Dynasty City. Based on the concept of Universal Studios in Hollywood, the facility doubles as a backlot for filming Chinese historical epics and a theme park where visitors can learn how movies are made. Meanwhile, American, European and Australian en-

tertainment companies are also gaining a foothold in Singapore. And they're making all kinds of things — feature films, television dramas, music videos, even Asian versions of popular European and American game shows.

Singapore's other theme parks are also taking the Hollywood route. Haw Par Villa — better known to generations of visitors as Tiger Balm Gardens — recently transformed itself from garish cement gardens into a high-tech Chinese mythological theme park. The attractions include a Wrath of the Gods flume ride, Spirits of the Orient Theatre and Tales of China boat ride — designed by an American firm that created theme parks in California and Florida.

Sentosa Island has also undertaken a mas-

sive metamorphosis with the addition of multiple new attractions and two new beach resorts called the Beaufort and Rasa Sentosa. In days gone by you could easily tour the theme park island in a single afternoon. But now it takes at least two days to see everything. Among the new temptations are a $20-million walk-through aquarium called Underwater World; an Asian cultural village featuring shops, restaurants and culture from around the region; and a water theme park with various slides and pools.

Rock stars, movie studios, theme parks —

Singapore is sounding more like Hollywood every day. People are even starting to act like this is California. Health food shops and aerobics classes are increasingly popular. Mountain bikes are *de rigueur* among a certain suburban set, and teenage skateboarders dodge pedestrians along Orchard Road. Singapore even has its own Hollywood-style "kiss and tell" books and a slightly racy tabloid called the *New Paper*.

Condos proliferate, self-proclaimed "bungalows in the sky" that come complete with swimming pools and tennis courts. There are long waiting lists for membership at exclusive domains like the Singapore Island Country Club and the Tanglin Club. And check the traffic outside the Turf Club on Saturday afternoons. Horse racing is one of the few forms

RIGHT: The Singapore Symphony Orchestra performs at the Victoria Concert Hall. A large part of the nation's thrust for cultural diversity is in the traditional Western performing arts such as symphony, ballet, opera and theatre.

Singapore is proud of its record of attracting established international artists. In addition, local companies continue to gain in skill and reputation. ABOVE: Conductor Choo Hoey of the Singapore Symphony.

of legal gambling in Singapore and there is rarely an empty seat in the house.

And much like Angelinos, the good citizens of Singapore spend much of their time dashing around in cars. Benzes, Beamers and Jaguars vie for space on the more fashionable residential streets. People zip around town on the most efficient and best maintained freeway system this side of the San Andreas Fault. Many cars are equipped with telephones and compact disk players. Some are even wired for personal computers. And if that's too high-

ABOVE LEFT: Haw Par Villa, better known as Tiger Balm Gardens, has been transformed into a high-tech Chinese mythological theme park, but not at the expense of its off-the-wall plaster sculptures. Among the new attractions are the Tales of China boat road, Wrath of the Gods flume ride and Creation of the World Theatre. LEFT: The childrens' gallery at the Singapore Science Centre with hands-on exhibits for youngsters.

Dinosaurs

The large dinosaurs or giants Triassic of Jurassic and Cretaceous era 190-64 metre years ago were the largest land creature ever to have lived.

Please do not step in

ABOVE: In keeping with Asia's reputation for larger-than-life monsters (a.k.a. Godzilla), the Singapore Science Centre features its own prehistoric beast. But it also has an Omni Theatre and Aviation Gallery that examines the concept of both earth and space flight.

RIGHT: A day at the races is popular, especially Saturday afternoons at the Bukit Turf Club. Founded in 1842, the track is among the oldest horseracing facilities in Asia. Biggest purses of the year are the Singapore Derby, Singapore Gold Cup and Queen Elizabeth II Cup. In keeping with the Singaporean penchant for food, the turf club has its own hawker centre, the Rasa Singapura. FAR RIGHT: Locals are equally crazy about golf. The island sports Asia's best selection of public and private courses. King of the links is the Singapore Island Country Club.

tech, there's always good old radio, a plethora of new stations that have sprung up in the 90s. Flip up and down the dial: at any given time you can catch opera, heavy metal, classic country or rap, with DJs that speak English, Mandarin, Tamil and Malay — radio that's every bit as multi-cultural as the country itself.

Live music is also expanding as local tastes become more eclectic and as Singaporeans bring back exotic audio appetites after business trips and student stints abroad. Orchard Road is lined with live music clubs. You can rub shoulders with Ameri-

can oil workers at a smokey country-western bar called Ginivy as couples dance the Texas two-step to the sound of a Filipino cowboy band. Rock'n'roll fans gets their kicks, not on route 66, but at Hard Rock Cafe. It has the best burgers in town in tune with an historic rock guitar collection and a black corset once worn on stage by sultry Anita Sarawak — Asian's answer to Tina Turner. The "world beat" predominates at Fabrice's, where you can shake your booty to the sound of Brazil samba, Jamaican reggae or South African township jive on any given night. Further down the road is Saxophone Bar, which attracts some of the world's top jazz artists despite the fact that it holds no more than a couple of dozen people.

The party continues down along Boat Quay, an historic riverside neighbourhood that's been re-cast into Singapore's most popular after-dark hangout. Al fresco dining in outdoor cafes along the waterfront is the most enticing attraction here, a startling array of eateries that includes Chinese, Indian and Malay food, as well as popular European delights. There's loads of *après* dinner entertainment — jazz at Harry's Bar, "unplugged" acoustic music at Off Quay, and irreverent Australian stand-up comedy at the Riverbank Pub.

But don't be lured into thinking that Singapore's nightlife is all pop schlock. The Singapore Symphony is one of Asia's best, with performances at

the Victoria Theatre that often feature guest conductors or solo artists from overseas. Chinese classics and folk music is the hallmark of the Singapore Broadcast Corp's Chinese Orchestra, and traditional Chinese music can also be heard at performances of Chinese opera staged at various venues, particularly during Chinese festivals.

Drama is still in its infancy, but a growing number of local companies are staging impressive works by both foreign and local playwrights. In fact, Singapore has become something of an Asian pioneer in offbeat theatre. TheatreWorks was one of the first Asian companies to produce the controversial *M Butterfly* — complete with nude scenes — and the avant-garde troupe offers an ongoing menu of unique drama at the Black Box Theatre in Fort Canning Park.

RIGHT: **If you're going to clone California, then you've gotta have theme parks. Singapore's favourite is Sentosa Island, which has a more eclectic selection than most. Besides a monorail and cable car ride, the island boasts a musical fountain, swimming lagoon, aquarium, live butterfly enclosure, rare** stone museum, maritime collection and — best of all — the superb Pioneers of Singapore exhibit and Surrender Chamber. ABOVE: **Surfs up! Sort of. Singapore's most popular beaches are at Changi and Sentosa, but the best are on Kusu and Sisters islands.**

CHAPTER TEN

THE FESTIVAL FIXATION

Crowds gather on the narrow lanes of Chinatown for the Lunar New Year fest. This is Singapore's most portentous — and longest —festival, with events spanning nearly a month in either January or February. All of Singapore is illuminated at this time, with gaily coloured lights and decorations. Lucky money called *hong bao* is given out to youngsters, while adults exchange traditional gifts such as tiny mandarin orange trees and chrysanthemums.

 Every day is a party in Singapore. Well, almost every day. For the island republic has the advantage of drawing its festive occasions from four distinct religious cultures, as well as its own history. Special events range from local temple festivals in which only a few hundred people take part, to nationwide celebrations attended by half a million or more people.

Traditional start of the festive year is Chinese New Year, which normally falls in late January or February. Celebrations tend to span about a month, but the culmination is always the colourful Chingay Parade down Orchard Road.

Thaipusam, one of the highlights of the Indian festival year, is an awe-inspiring demonstration of faith and courage: devotees endure great pain and suffering as they march between Singapore's two most notable Hindu shrines.

For Malays, the most significant time of year is Ramadan — the Muslim month of fasting — and the subsequent Hari Raya celebrations once the fast is over. These usually fall in the April to June period, depending on the lunar cycle like so many Singapore festivals.

The biggest secular celebration is National Day on 9th August, which is celebrated with a parade along the Padang or a spectacular show in the National Stadium.

OPPOSITE: The colourful Chingay Procession down Orchard Road is the highlight of the Lunar New Year. You don't have to be Chinese to join in, for Singaporeans of all races and creeds join in, donning fantastic costumes reminiscent of Carnival in Rio. These participants are Chinese stilt walkers. LEFT: Fast and furious action from the International Dragon Boat Festival, staged in late May or early June on Marina Bay. ABOVE: The menacing dragon is familiar at all Chinese festivals.

One of Singapore's more unusual annual religious events is the Festival of the Nine Emperor Gods, held in late October or early November. This particular pantheon of Taoist gods are known for their curative powers, in addition to granting long life and good fortune. RIGHT: Lost in a trance, a female priest pleads to the gods. LEFT: Culmination of the festival is a spirited procession in which effigies of the gods are carried on sedan chairs across burning hot offerings.

LEFT: **A rare performance of traditional Fukkien string puppets during a temple festival in Chinatown.**

ABOVE: **Chinese opera is not indigenous to any one festival; it can usually be found at any large Chinese celebration or special event. These troupes are the Erwoo Group (top) and the Chinese Theatre Circle (bottom).**

Thaipusam is the island's most conspicuous Indian festival. This is a test of faith and courage, two virtues displayed in what outsiders consider rather gruesome fashion. Devotees pierce their bodies and faces with sharp metal hooks or pins (below), then place heavy metal cages called *kavadis* on their shoulders; these in turn are attached to the hooks and pins (right). Sometimes, devotees will drag a heavy Honda generator behind them to provide power for an illuminated *kavadi*. Their procession winds from the Perumal Temple on Serangoon Road to the Chettiar Temple on Tank Road.

Sultan Mosque in Kampong Glam comes alive with bright lights during the post-Ramadan celebration called Hari Raya. Ramadan is Islam's month of fasting and prayer. Muslims refrain from eating during the daylight hours, but at night they feast upon sumptuous meals prepared at home or in outdoor cafes around the city.

The autumn Lantern Festival
is another time of bright
illuminations in Singapore.
The festivities are best
watched at the Chinese
Garden in Jurong (left and
above). But all around town,
people hang chromatic paper
lanterns, in traditional
Chinese designs or more
modern formats like boats,
planes and trains.

One people, one nation, one Singapore: everyone comes together at the National Stadium or the Padang for independence celebrations on 9th August. The extravaganza normally combines cultural performances such as ethnic dances and music, with overt military touches like a shrieking fly-past of air force fighter jets or an olive-green column of tanks and armoured personnel carriers.

INDEX

ACKNOWLEDGEMENTS

Tan Bee Choo; Joan Lloyd; Molly Tay;
Raffles Hotel (1886) Pte. Ltd; Larry Yeo and
Antiques of the Orient Gallery;
Juanita Shakila and Nelli Yong of the
Westin Stamford Hotel; Sherman Tan;
Eric Tay, James Nah and the third year
graphic design students of
Temasek Polytechnic; Dorothy Kannan and
Darrell Bay of Design Objectives;
Lorrain Chong and Kevin Dragon of the
Singapore Tourist Promotion Board.

JOHOR BAHRU

CAUSEWAY

WOODLANDS

KRANJI
RESERVOIR

ZOOLOGICAL
GARDENS

LIM CHU KANG

SELETA
RESER

MANDAI ORCHID
GARDEN

CHOA CHU KANG

PEIRCE RESE

CHINESE
GARDEN

TANG DYNASTY
VILLAGE

BOTANIC
GARDENS

JURONG
INDUSTRIAL ESTATE

JURONG
BIRD PARK

ORCHARD
ROAD

HAW PAR
VILLA